W9-BIY-736

INTIMATE LETTERS
OF
JAMES GIBBONS HUNEKER

Major CRITIC
+ ESSAYIST

JAMES HUNEKER (aged 54)

From a photograph taken in Berlin

INTIMATE LETTERS

OF

JAMES GIBBONS HUNEKER

COLLECTED AND EDITED BY

Josephine Huneker

WITH A FOREWORD BY
BENJAMIN DeCASSERES

LIVERIGHT PUBLISHING CORP.
NEW YORK

DEDICATED
TO
ALL THE TRUE FRIENDS
OF
JAMES GIBBONS HUNEKER

ILLUSTRATIONS

FOREWORD

Buffon's "The style is the man himself" is one of those generalizations that are only applicable to the exceptions.

Some styles merely indicate certain traits of the writer, some styles are masks to hide entirely the personality—indeed, the very character of the writer.

It is a commonplace that almost all writers in their personal lives bear no resemblance to the image we conceive of them from their poems or prose.

But there are rare instances—and James Gibbons Huneker was one of them—where the style is the very spit and spawn of the man.

These few men literally *live* while they are writing. In Huneker the co-ordination between the man, his thought, his style, his speech, his very manner of drinking a seidel of Pilsner, was perfect.

His face was his style. His work was his style. His conversational manner was his style.

His face was ironic, forceful, Goethean. His walk—his carriage—was chip-on-the shoulder, the carriage and walk of a Challenger. His talk was electric, epigrammatic, obscene, direct, and sometimes flavored with a subtle genial diabolism.

All these traits are in the style of this our greatest critic of the arts, a man who stands absolutely alone in American letters, a man who had no predecessor and who has had no successor.

There was also in Huneker at times a curious timidity, a kind of humility, a kind of shamefacedness at his own greatness and cultural depths, which those who did not know him as well as I did might have taken for egotistical hypocrisy.

But it was really part of the innate character of the man.

Genius in America when it mixes with mediocrities—and Huneker was a superb mixer—is compelled to shield itself, to assume a mask, to hide itself, to take on the protective coloring of the crowd.

But when Huneker was among his own—poets, artists, social and artistic rebels, musical composers and painters of the rare and the individual—he was in full bloom.

He was thus a man who literally *lives* in his letters and works. So much so that when I re-read his essays and letters fifteen years after his death he comes before me as if alive.

In these letters and essays I hear his voice and see his gestures again. He is materialized for me as completely as if he stood before me—I carry on with him in his work those innumerable conversations which were in his lifetime non-stop talks, many times, from dusk to dawn.

Vibrant, electric, spontaneous, discursive, casual, cater-cornered in life, one page of his writings evokes for me his personality.

So powerfully has this phenomenon worked in me at times that I look up suddenly from his printed letters, his "Steeplejack" or from some of his essays and involuntarily salute him with an "Hello, Jim!"

I had corresponded with him from 1901 to 1908, when one morning in the latter year, at about 3 o'clock, I met him in Jack's restaurant. I introduced myself. He rose from his chair, and, with a seidel of Pilsner in one hand and pointing the other directly at me, thundered:

"Schopenhauer or Nietzsche?"

The last time I was with him was shortly before his death in 1921. I met him on Park Row. Again he pointed a finger at me and boomed:

"What do you think of this — Eighteenth Amendment?"

This was characteristic of Jim. On meeting you, no commonplaces, no "How are you?" or "Fine day!" It

FOREWORD

was always a sudden explosion about art, literature, philosophy or drink.

This living Huneker you will find in these "Intimate Letters"—a splendid title, for Huneker was always intimate.

Nearly all of them begin with a bang! Except when writing to his editor, no "Dear Sir" stuff. They reek with colloquialisms, puns, sudden incisive judgments, slaps on the shoulder, vivid snapshots of personalities far and near, Rabelaisian *mots,* confessions and parenthetical remarks (he had a parenthetical mind—a mind that was pulled hither and thither by an associative apparatus in his brain that dragged up bizarre and curious bucketfuls of cultural and ideological fish from the subconscious).

Huneker was the farthest removed from the stilted, the pedantic and the academic of any writer who has lived among us.

All his letters are collaborations of Huneker and the man or woman to whom he is writing.

Huneker was, in fact, primarily a collaborator—like Montaigne and Remy de Gourmont, for instance.

He collaborated with life, with the universe. To use the jargon of professors, he was subjective—intensely subjective. He fused his ego with the person he was writing about— Nietzsche, Flaubert, Poe, Liszt, Rembrandt, Stirner, Degas, Goya, Chopin, Huysmans, Baudelaire.

No matter what or whom he was writing about he was writing about Huneker. He saw all genius as one of the facets of himself.

For this reason all his work is creative, vital, dynamic. He put the full power of an unshackled individualism into every line he wrote.

Not that he couldn't be objective. His objectivity was founded on an innate organ of *taste* second to no man writing in this century. He knew the genuine from the quack, an original from a faker, a genius from a *poseur* instantaneously.

FOREWORD

In conversation he sometimes summed up, and shattered, a celebrity in a single word.

I recall "How pretty!" in regard to the work of a famous painter, "gargle!" in regard to the work of a poet who was the vogue, "for ladies only" about a novelist touted by the reviewers as a "Second Balzac," "frozen gonads" about a "philosopher."

These fascinating letters—each one of which is a pungent slice of Huneker himself and collectively are a mosaic of a Huneker who always contradicted a Huneker, but who was consistent with his Daimon—these letters begin in 1900 and end in 1921.

These twenty-one years span Huneker's most productive years, the years that saw his rise to fame, the years from Chopin (1900) to "Variations" (1921).

And what a parade of genius Huneker led across the arid minds of America lined with literary bumwad in those twenty-one years!—Chopin, Brahms, Richard Strauss, Wagner, Balzac, Flaubert, Nietzsche, George Moore, Gorky, Duse, Strindberg, Ibsen, Bernard Shaw, D'Annunzio, Maeterlinck, Stendhal, Cézanne, Carrière, Daumier, El Greco, Lafcadio Hearn, Joseph Conrad, Wedekind—but the list is interminable. For it was Huneker who introduced Europe to America and did more than any man in America to smash the strangle-hold of the Puritan garrotters on our literature.

Huneker did not clear the air in America of professorial nunkey-donkeyism and Puritanical hypocrisy and smugness by direct attacks.

He attacked the spawn of "Godey's Lady's Book," whose violent blushes in the presence of sex and revolutionary artistic ideas extended even unto Howells and Twain, from *behind*—the proper place to attack Moralic Smugness in the arts as well as in actual life.

He broke down our provincialism by erosion—the erosion of European culture, which he heaped on America in season and out, or, as Huneker once said, "Yankees win or Yankees lose, I announce Chopin, Flaubert, Stendhal and Company!"

Just before he died the stench of what Remy de Gourmont calls "factory-smoke literature" began to assail his delicate intellectual nostrils. It was coeval (and co-evil) with Prohibition and Russian Communism.

Huneker, although the most catholic of critics in his tastes, insisted that no matter what you wrote about it had to be *literature*, it had to have quality. The "school," the "movement" you belonged to in music, painting or writing wasn't of the slightest importance to Huneker. "Do you know your business; are you doing a good job?" was all he asked.

He was himself an aristocrat, and, like all real aristocrats, thoroughly democratic. In one day he could write an essay on Nietzsche, hold a conversation with a cop or a bartender in the latter's own lingo, empty a seidel of beer over de Pachmann's head (which he actually did in Lüchow's), struggle with the intricacies of the Second Ballade of Chopin on his piano, and then write a two-column article for a newspaper on Arkansas cyclones (which he also actually did for the *World*).

Wherever Huneker went he was immediately surrounded by all kinds of persons. His glowing, incandescent personality drew around him all the moths of theatre and opera lobbies, bars and cafés.

He knew the Fifth Avenue traffic cops and many of the bartenders in New York by name. He knew all the great beer-routes in Europe, just as he knew the history and the work of every artist, writer and musician who had ever got on paper or canvas.

Men like Herbert Spencer and John Stuart Mill made him sick at the stomach.

He had no use for strong spirits. Bacchus and Gambrinus were his gods.

He had a great admiration for the Jews—he loved them.

FOREWORD

He deplored the fact that he had not a "drop of that precious Semitic blood in my veins."

He was, in politics, a furious enemy of regimentation of any kind. "Let them go," he said to me one day in 1920 in speaking about Lenin and Trotsky; "they'll pave the way for Individual Anarchy!"

Upon the original publication of these "Intimate Letters" in 1924, although no reviews of the volume were printed, personal criticism was made against the various individuals concerned with the editing and publishing of this work.

Such criticism was based upon complete misunderstanding of the purpose of the book, together with a lack of knowledge of the personality of the author.

And the friends of James Huneker owe a debt to T. R. Smith for his efforts in bringing forth this volume and re-printing it in a day of cafeteria culture and "factory smoke literature."

It might be said of these letters of Huneker's what Walt Whitman said of Leaves of Grass, "Whoso touches this book touches a Man."

August, 1936.   BENJAMIN DeCASSERES.

< 1900 >

INTIMATE LETTERS OF
JAMES GIBBONS HUNEKER

To Henry T. Finck

May 28, 1900
19 Union Square, West.

MY DEAR HENRY:

You are really to be pitied, spitted as you are on the fork of friendship. *The Book Buyer*, the *Evening Post* and the *Bookman*—for Prof. Peck tells me you have been kind enough to do the Chopin *there*—doesn't it make you very tired? And you the original Chopinist of us all! Really old man you are very good to me, and always have been and in these lonesome latter days of mine your words, printed and otherwise, have been tonic for me. *Encore* thanks! Pray present my regards to Madame Finck; I hope you both will have a charming Summer. I've deserted music—besides the daily grind and fugitive articles—for many years. I *study* piano for the good of my soul and oddly enough Chopin, not Brahms. It is a wise preacher who can swallow his own sermons! My short stories will be out, I hope, in February next. Then fiction forever!

As ever your friend,

Henry T. Finck.   JIM.

To E. E. Ziegler

The Carrollton, 981 Madison Ave., N. Y.
Aug. 23rd, 9:30 p.m., 1900.

DEAR NED:

I'm sorry you missed my wire, for I wanted to see you tonight. I'm also sorry my letter hurt you; it was not meant to be harsh. I needed the books. But don't bother about them now—it's too late. Thanks for Reuben and Stevenson; I'm loaded with lore to the guards. Now when you get this, go over to the Carrollton: the elevator boy will give you 7 books and 4 weeklies. 5 of the books are Balzac's; the other 2 are Reuben and Hannah Smith. Read the logic of "Style"; it is very stimulating and sound to the core—yet difficult reading withal. Keep the Balzacs and those other 4 books until I return in October. I waited today for you at the office, but had so much to do that I left at 11.30. The pot was boiling tonight for you, but you did not turn up. I am sorry. My address until Sep. 15 is The Oceanic, Isle of Shoals, off Portsmouth, N. H. I'll acquaint you with our later address. I'll be in Worcester Sep. 26-28. We leave tomorrow—Friday—on the limited for Boston, 10 a. m. Expect to reach Grand Central Depot at 9.30—in the New Haven and Hartford waiting room. If you get this in time—an A. D. T. pup promises to post it—run down. That is, of course, if you feel like it. I hate to leave without saying goodbye, especially as you seem put out about a very unimportant matter.

Au Revoir—Papa (?)!!!

As ever

JAMES.

The Missus sends regards and Adieux.

E. E. Ziegler

To E. E. Ziegler

The Waumbek, Jefferson, New Hampshire,
Sep. 8, 1900

A—Chos—! Ker-Chos!!!

How do you do, Ned? I'm miserable, thanks. Had to leave Isle of Fools or Aisle of Shoals because of hay fever and leave here Monday because of hay fever. Everyone plays golf at this very swell hostelry—plays golf and sneezes. So my new address will be "The Maplewood," Maplewood, N. H. It is near Bethlehem, and I had perfect relief last year. I'm sorry you are not in good spirits, though to be sure there is no particular reason why you should be. Cheer up! Cherries are ripe now. I rec'd both your letters, and hasten to thank you—48 hours late—for your amiability. Don't read too much. I've done little except "Faust" and Ibsen. Had to write a Nietzsche Ed. for *M. C.* without my reference books except the Baker-Schirmer Musical Dictionary for

bare dates of birth, &c. So the article must read
nice! "Little Dancer" for "a lithe dancer," not to
mention queer punctuation; it was a strain on my
memory, I tell you. Try to get a comfortable place
to live in. For many reasons I'm sorry you left
Mrs. O. You were looked after there. Don't read
too much. It's a mistake. Don't read anything
written after 1800. You are right. Damn the
moderns! I've been very sick—sneeze, spit and
swear! I go 26 inst. to Worcester. Hale will be
there. Likewise Krehbiel.

As ever

E. E. Ziegler.   JIM.

To E. E. Ziegler

Maplewood, N. H., Sep. 24, 1900

MY DEAR NED:

I hasten to answer yours received just now. I do
not know the man you mention, nor do I know any
one that does. Why not go on and ask boldly for the
job? It succeeds sometimes, and if you get it you
won't keep it long—you could never stand that office
or those people. However, don't mind me, and try,
and if you care to use my name as a reference, in
this or any analogous case, use it freely and often.
My address is Worcester after tomorrow—Tuesday.
Will be Bay State House—I stay there until Friday

sometime. I'll see you next week after Monday. I hate to return, so lovely is this place, the mountains, air, &c. I've read nothing but big books, Goethe, Milton, Browne, Tolstoi, all the poets and Don Quixote. The latter is still a unicum; it is hopelessly unapproachable as a story, as a colored narrative. The moderns with their subtle spinnings, their damned psychology, and soul-belly aching, seem petty trimmers and mouthers. I hope you are nicely settled. Chilton writes me he "likes you"; that's easy. Everyone does that, my laddy buck, only your modesty gets in your way.

As ever

JIM.

With regards from the Missus. I'm afraid I've got to do "the English opera for *T. T.!* Brentano sent me "The Idiot," and I am to expect "The Gambler" next.

E. E. Ziegler.

To Mrs. Charles H. Ditson

New York, 981 Madison Ave.
Thursday, 1901

MY DEAR MRS. DITSON:

I tried to phone you yesterday, but could not catch you. I then promised myself to call after a "Hamlet" matinee, on the East Side, but a fire broke out at the Antoinette where my brother Paul's wife lives, and of course, I had to "run with the engine." Just now I would "run" with anything to forget the vile theatres! I can't call before Saturday morning. I have 97 matinees every day, more or less. How would Saturday do, at noon! The afternoon is to be given over to my real sister from Philadelphia. Indeed, Mrs. Ditson, I am so out of music, and so provincial of late, that the moss is growing in my ears. I no longer regard life as a sound, but as a smell.

Sincerely your Admirer
(a bashful one)
JAMES HUNEKER.

Mrs. Charles H. Ditson.

To Mme. Frida Ashforth

April 21, 1901

MY DEAR LADY FRIDA:

Thanks for your kind words. I did the best I could. Mr. B. was very good to print the article and

picture—don't you think so? I thought of putting in
your name with the Steins, Bleiers and Fleisch-
manns, but concluded that it might be misinterpreted.
Everyone knows that if it had not been for you, poor
Al would have been dead long ago.

I haven't the heart to tell you about the funeral.
No one, not a soul of his friends, actors, musicians
or newspapermen, was there. Mr. Stein, Ben Bleier,
a Mr. Bailey—old school friend—a Mr. Willimoot—
unknown to me—and William Grevel, of the Vienna
Bakery—myself. Not another man. Mrs. E. Fried-
berg, his aunt, turned up and cried terribly—aunts
always do at funerals. I tell you, Frida, it was the
saddest thing I ever went through. Poor Al, not
weighing 60 pounds, was put on a platter like a
duck to be roasted and pushed into the furnace. So
ends a sad life! I wonder why Edgar Levey, Edgar
Saltus—why the gang didn't turn up? I was glad
to see that *Town Topics* gave the actors and musicians
a hard knock, but even the writer Nirdlinger did not
put in an appearance. The De Reszkes wired flow-
ers, and so did Lawrence Reamer. I hope to see you
before you sail. I've been terribly depressed the
past three or four days, remaining indoors. I can't
forget that lonely little coffin!

As ever

Jim.

Mme. Frida Ashforth.

To Henry B. Fuller

981 Madison Ave., N. Y.
May 11, 1902

MY DEAR MR. FULLER:

I was not in the city when your kind letter arrived. Let me hasten to thank you for your trouble. Volney Streamer suggested sending the little volume— you are to blame partially, for its publication; your letter in 1896 set me working, and it was not, I assure you, with the idea of a review that "Melomaniacs" was mailed. There are few people on the rind of this planet whose praise is dear to me. Hence your words were deeply appreciated. It is always the disciple addressing the master when I write you. I realized this but an hour ago, when I read your magnificently subtle "At Saint Judas."

Sincerely,
JAMES HUNEKER.

Henry B. Fuller.

To Benjamin De Casseres

981 Madison Ave.
Dec. 14, 1902

MY DEAR MR. DE CASSERES:

Thank you so much for the magazine. I read your article with much pleasure, and I recall with particular interest the study of Hardy's women. My wife

cut it out and gave it to me some time ago.   As for
Wilshire's I think the magazine all right.   My friend
Mr. John Graham Brooks, of Boston, writes for it.
He is an *advanced* Socialist, *i.e.*, that means individu-
alist—the only religion for a man with brains and
character.   When the season begins to wither, can't
we meet for a spell of talk and a drink!   Some place
on the East Side, where the wine is anarchy breeding, the surrounding evocative of conspiracy!   I have
a bad cold—hence these morbid notions.

Sincerely
JAMES HUNEKER.

P. S.—If you ever have to look at my "Melomaniacs," short stories printed by Scribner's, you will
find a new version of anarchy in the tale called "A
Piper of Dreams."   It describes the destruction of
the state by—music, dear, sweet, innocent music, the
most evil weapon—the devil (?) ever employed.

Benj. De Casseres.

To Benjamin De Casseres

The Carrollton, 981 Madison Ave., N. Y.
April 10, 1903

LIEBER HERR CASSERES:

"Syncopated Spider" is good, is more than good. Where in the name of the great Verbal Beelzebub did you get it? I envy it. I shall quote it. Thanks for the *critic*—which I had seen, read, marked, enjoyed. I may only say that your style has something of the brilliant, crackling, fulminating quality of Carlyle— a Carlyle who has read Nietzsche. I hope to see you before I sail for Europe—and more critical toil.

Sincerely, as ever
JAMES HUNEKER.

Benj. De Casseres.

To Mrs. Charles H. Ditson

New York, 981 Madison Ave.
Nov. 14, 1903

MY DEAR MRS. DITSON:

Pen in hand, and cigarette in the other (other hand), I inscribe my thanks. I never smoked a cigarette before in my life. I am a rank heretic on the subject—I mean I was—you have converted me! If you see a narrow-chested, puny person on the Avenue who bows to you in an idiotic expression—

c'est moi! I am a cigarette "fiend" from this time
on. *You* are to blame.

Thanks all the same.

Sincerely,
JAMES HUNEKER.

Mrs. Charles H. Ditson.

To E. E. Ziegler

Dresden, June 24, 1903

DEAR BILL:

Had an awful time in Leipzig, hunting the Wagner
house in the *Perühl,* not a soul ever heard of Wagner!! Found it at last, No. 3, with an old commem-
orative bust—worth 2 marks. Saw Gewandhaus and
Auerbad, &c. Also all the hospitals—the driver took
me for a scab expert. But Dresden! The Gallery—
Mein Gott! Off to Vienna at noon.

As ever
JIM.

The Missus will never, never go to Europe again.
The pace has been too killing. I have the gout—am
drinking Rhenser water.

E. E. Ziegler.

(Post Card)

< 1904 >

To Henry T. Finck

(Confidential)

981 Madison Ave.
February 1st, 1904

DEAR HARRY:

We may disagree about Parsifal, Richard Strauss, Brahms *et al;* but we do shake hands on Liszt's music. This apropos of your comprehensive and acute notice of Philharmonic Concert last Saturday. The *pattern* of the concerto is wonderful, so wonderful, so logical, so closely spun, so brilliant in pattern that his formal magnificence is always overlooked. It is called a rhapsody, fantasy—as if the last Sonatas of Beethoven are not infinitely more fantastic in feeling, looser in texture! But there—you know all this; said all this. What I wrote for is to tell you that I really enjoyed your notice of Reisenauer. And while everyone noticed the marvellous little transitional modulation between concerto and chant Polonaise, none but you wrote of it. Wasn't it delightful? He took the eloquent *appoggiatura* of Liszt, transformed its rhythm and presently we were in a mazurka! I so seldom go to concerts—the first in two years—and so seldom read music criticism that when I get a satisfactory installment of both I slop over. Forgive the past, Father Finck, and receive a sinner in the fold (though I dislike Parsifal more than ever). Some day I shall use—with your per-

mission of course—that extremely interesting Seidl
letter from Bayreuth which you printed in the *Post*
last week.   By the way I have come upon a detail
of Liszt's music which astounded me so that I am
still bowled over by it.   I shall keep it for your
private ear.   To discover it I went through all the
scores bar by bar of Wagner, Chopin, Tschaikowsky,
Schumann, Berlioz and Strauss—and Liszt is ahead
of the whole crowd in—I'll keep the secret for a
while!   Amazing it is, I assure you.   It cost me
much labor.   Yet, Henry, Liszt is *not* Wagner and
the borrowings don't count for a damn any more than
do Shakespeare's indiscriminate pilferings from Hol-
inshed, Montaigne, Plutarch, Bandello, &c.   All of
which I intend putting into print some day.   Tell
Mrs. Finck that *we* are hopeless—but as soon as the
season thins down we shall both call.   How is Mr.
Towse?   He is the sanest critic of drama in America.
   With regards from haus zu haus
                   As ever
Henry T. Finck.   JIM HUNEKER.

To Henry T. Finck

                   981 Madison Ave., N. Y.
                   March 8, 1904
DEAR HARRY:
   Your letter grieved me, for after 20 years' friend-
ship it is not pleasant to be misunderstood.   I am

not an apostle for anyone; I haven't, and never had
any ambitions in the critical line. If my publishers
call me an "authority" that is their affair. You
were not only the first *Chopin* apostle, but also the
first *Liszt*, the first *Wagner* in America! Now, honestly old man have I ever tried to steal another
man's thunder, when have I refused to credit *you*
with all you deserve? You might remember when
I was on the *Courier* how I quoted you as an authority! As for Strauss—I know him slightly; his
personality is not appealing. He has been wofully
treated here, the result I presume of his surround-
ings—I have heard him conduct "Tristan" in Berlin masterfully, and later his own music indiffer-
ently. No, I am not going to the Liederkranz, I
never go to dinners public or private; I haven't the
time; as for making a speech—Mein *Gott!* Heinrich,
is that a little joke? I couldn't say five words on
my hind-legs. No, my *Parsifal* article is not—except for a paragraph—the same stuff in the *Metropolitan.* You must think I'm mad! I've written
12,000 words, serious, dignified and I hope analytic,
praising and censuring the work. I was enraged
to see music like "Tristan" neglected for the *Parsifal*
circus; hence my rather noisy and too pungent attack. You know I love Wagner too much not to
revolt at certain methods of praising him, uncritical
and vulgar, by the younger generation! (By the
way, shall I answer that Goepp letter in the *Post?*)

Not only, my dear fellow, will your name be credited as the *first* and *only* critic in this country and among the first in Europe who stood out for Liszt—hang it all, I am one of your converts; but in my Parsifal I quote you as the best biographer Wagner ever had in English—and I might have added truthfully in German, too, for I am no *Schwärmer* for Glasenapp or Houston Chamberlain; however, the general scope of the study did not necessitate my saying the latter. I asked you several years ago why you didn't "do" a Liszt! I still marvel you did not. I'm damnably sorry I ever began; his church music alone is colossal. My little new volume of essays is nothing but a "flyer." I am done, absolutely, with musical essays after my Liszt. I loathe criticism! I wish to do something original, individual. I have written a little study of Nietzsche-Wagner in "Overtones," in which I side with Wagner. Nietzsche was a hopeless man to live with. There is a second Wagner essay, and in the Strauss study—13,000 words—I have modified several exaggerated passages which appeared in *Scribner's*. I am sorry you don't care for Strauss— he is a true Lisztianer and a real descendant of the great Franz.

Now after these long-winded explanations, Henry, my boy, I do hope you will realize my position. I am through with music criticism; I aspire for man's honors. I always credit where I can; and I am still an admirer of one *H. T. Finck* who taught me a lot in my life—I am not a hero worshipper—except of Seidl, Paderewski and Joseffy; I go to no banquets and—perhaps my Parsifal study will please you after all. If you don't like "Overtones" say so;—give it the devil; but read it! you will probably disagree with every chapter. Our regards to Mrs. Finck. And believe me, your old friend through thick and thin.

JIM.

To Benjamin De Casseres

The Carrollton, 981 Madison
March 21, 1904

For heaven's sake, my dear Mr. De Casseres, don't think that I have been trying to play the pedagogue— I have too many sins to answer for on my own account. What I meant was that your style so condensed, so weighty, so meaty, is difficult for the *hoi polloi*. Of course it's you—no one else. Without reading your name at the end of the article, without reading the lines, I can tell you at an arm's length simply by the spacing, paragraphing, &c. But you are young, in the Orphic mood. It will wear away. Pessimism will prove as empty as Optimism—nothing is really worth while but the brain—the emotions are rank swindles. If a man possesses his skull, he is master of the stars.   (I am in the De Casseres key, myself, just now!)

"Overtones" is largely journalism—the "Nietz-sche" will disappoint you.   It was written in 1896 or 1897.   It is *popular*.   You don't suppose that *I* would be allowed to print the truth about N.!!!   I think I can attract more readers for him by stating in pleas-ing, superficial terms to the general reader (dear old G. R.!) what Nietzsche stood for; in a word play the role of popularizer.   Many people believe he threw benzine at priests, or spat on ladies' dresses, or some wild fables.   I am a Roman Catholic, was educated for the priesthood, so I know, I hear of the vile lies circulated about a great soul.   I went to Weimar last summer to see his sister; also to Naum-burg.   The man's life was nobility itself; a hater of the vulgar, of cheap journalism, of facile writing. A pessimist not in the sour-bellied Schopenhauerian sense, but a pessimist with a divinely discontented soul.

I heard Joseffy play Saturday afternoon with the Boston Symphony orchestra; all my old love for the ideal music came back with typhoonic force.   I've been unhappy ever since.   I play the piano 2 hours every day, rain or shine, but Joseffy—it is the ideal presentation of an ideal.   Such a man confutes phi-losophies with a touch.   There is a neat little pamph-let new to me, published by Macmillan & Co., entitled "The Philosophy of Friedrich Nietzsche," by Grace

Neal Dolsen. It costs 75 cts. It is by a woman who possesses synthetic ability, and best of all, it contains an excellent bibliography; I can recommend it for its condensed facts.

Fraternally
JAMES HUNEKER.

Benjamin De Casseres.

To Henry T. Finck

(Confidential)

The Carrollton, 981 Madison Ave., N. Y.
March 22, 1904

DEAR HARRY:

Just a line to say that H. E. K. swears that Wagner *never* contemplated a drama in which Jesus was to figure with Magdalen tempting him. To be sure the temptation incident was eliminated from the scenario, but in Finck's "Wagner" vol. II. p. 398 the Frau Wille story is related. To this I referred Krehbiel. And if you are right, so am I! Mottl is the conductor who saw Wagner's autobiography at Bayreuth. You were right years ago; the matter if W. acknowledges his paternity—what a row! A mistake, inexcusable, but selbstverständlich occurs in "Overtones" p. 11. I meant to write "it is a rondo in form" (*i.e.* "Till" but "scherzo" got in and of course, it is a mistake. It will be corrected later.

I didn't bother answering in the *Post* that challenge of Goepp, for the reason that it was too easy to demolish him. In the legend or history *Till Eulenspiegel* escaped the gallows, in the Strauss score, he is gibbeted—though, as the epilogue proves by its themes, his spirit will always live. Besides what the devil's the difference anyhow? Ach, Heinrich, this is a queer world! I console myself now with Liszt letters— what a wilderness, what a mountain of correspondence, nuggets lying exposed in every letter!

As ever

JIM.

Henry T. Finck.

To Henry T. Finck

The Carrollton, 981 Madison Ave., N. Y.
March 25, 1904

DEAR HARRY:

Your letter was welcome. For heaven's sake don't bother about that damned book—it is, or was, a gelegenheits-stück, and not to be taken as a serious contribution to serious musical problems. To be quite outspoken I set more store by the Nietzsche, Balzac, Flaubert essays than the other polemical stuff. Balzac for a music-hater divined Richard Wagner, *he must have met him.* I had ordered the Berlioz study; thanks all the same for remembering me. After I heard Richard Strauss conduct the

"Faust" Symphony, "Orpheus" and "Les Preludes" of Liszt I went off my head about him. I asked him to accept the dedication of the life—but *I* changed my mind since. Yes, my boy, I not only read all the Liszt letters, new and old, but reviewed them to the extent of a hundred or more columns in the *Courier*, first in 1888—Wagner-Liszt—and later the La Mara bundle. But I'm re-reading them, Heinrich! I like to do things thoroughly. I have two years before my last proofs are to be handed in and I mean the job to be, if nothing else, a monument to my patience. I joke over it—and I love the work. What I am going to say is that L. is a *melodic* genius of the first rank. He has more natural melody than Wagner, and then my discovery —doesn't your mouth water? It's astounding! To get its full significance I have examined and am still examining the music of Liszt from his piano pieces to his symphonic works. Such a Treasure trove! What do I care if the book is cut up? when you're right, &c., &c. Strauss, my dear fellow, is a big fellow, bigger to me than Berlioz, whose music I loathe. It is all cerebral; while Strauss, in his songs, at least, shows heart and imagination. *You* don't go in a foot-note! What rot after your savage warfare for years in a cause that looked hopeless. In the matter of purely literary events the Liszt book threw up the most fascinating appeals to me—and, I confess, it is a danger that I must steer away from.

You suggested this in print, if I remember right.

By the way—I threw my cap in the air at Mac-Dowell's stand. It was noble, unselfish, and absolutely *ideal* in this money-grubbing age. The Bach book I have, indeed I have all Lisztiana—ask Ziegler, who weeps when he looks over my amassed material. I gave Scribner's *carte blanche*. And in Europe last summer I gobbled up lots of pamphlets &c. much to Mrs. Huneker's dismay and the trunk's discomfiture. Tretbar has put at my disposal 40 years of Breitkopf & Hartel's review—indexed. I shall read letter L. and find fresh stuff. In a word, not to bore you, my loins are girded up for the labor. Just to get my hand in I shall publish a book—not musical or fiction—next February and then pitch in.

I need hardly add that my unsocial behavior results from my crazy idea of getting through with what I started out to do. I really left music-criticism because I have only one third the labor I underwent in music journalism and leisure to myself —all day, every day in the week and most of the nights. I go nowhere, I no longer *Kniepp*—solid altogether. I miss you, though I read the *Post* every day. But thus it is—to do anything one must be selfish. Disgusting life. A ranch would be heaven. But I'll pull through somehow and then to fiction.

With regards to you and yours

As ever

Henry T. Finck.   JIM.

To Perriton Maxwell

981 Madison Avenue,
June 2nd, 1904

DEAR MR. MAXWELL:

From heaven to hell I soared and dove in my library, in my magazines, in my plays, in my letters but that damnable imp of a Shaw photograph eluded. Literally I have wasted my night. It is now 10.30 p. m. and I began the search at 5.30. I chuck it. The picture has, is vanished. Just like Shaw—he is always giving trouble. So I send you two substitutes; one caricature by Max Beerbohm which I have never seen in American reprints; the other, G. B. S. as he is. How about one or both? Also, can you use the Max cut? It appeared some years ago, 5 or 6, say, but where I know not. I fancy if it is credited at the bottom of the reproduction that it will be sufficient. But you know more about these things than I do. I think the caricature simply immense, don't you? The copy will be down by midday Monday.

Sincerely as ever

JAMES HUNEKER.

Perriton Maxwell.

P.S. I shall give one more search Tomorrow!

To Benjamin De Casseres

The Carrollton, 981 Madison Ave.
March 22, 1904

MY DEAR DE CASSERES:

You amaze me! You, too, a Philadelphian, and a friend of Joe Gibbons, who was my playmate and favorite cousin. I haven't seen him for years. *He* will tell you I was destined for the priesthood, but having more than brains, it was concluded that I had better stick to a secular profession. Of course, I'm a Catholic. Aren't you? There was a De Casseres family in Philadelphia, but they were Jews. Do *you* belong to that branch? After having proved Richard Wagner half Jew in "Overtones," I am ready to call the whole world Hebraic—so pardon my impertinent curiosity.

The essay *hat geschmäckt*. I shall keep it by me and quote it—with credit—perhaps next Sunday. We must surely arrange for a meeting some Saturday in May, when I shall feel freer. Do you agree? Just the two—and let us drink tea, not mention Jesus, and thresh out the universe. I wish you could see my library! I cry sometimes at the thought of dying—for then in the great Inane, I shall have to leave my books.   Fraternally,

J. H.

Just received a letter from Ben Tucker, the Anarchist.

To Henry T. Finck

981 Madison Ave., N. Y.
January 8, 1905

DEAR HARRY:

Only a line to tell you that I enjoyed—if one dare enjoy an obituary—your notice of Theodore Thomas in the *Post* last week. That New York allowed such a man to go to Chicago is its lasting disgrace. I was glad to see you put the truth on paper with such an unmistakable sincerity. How are you? I was in Weimar a long time. Have all material now at hand for Liszt. I intend calling on you next Spring, late, for data as I purpose writing your name more than once in the study. A hellish job. Coward! Shirker! Lazybones! It's your work I'm attempting! I particularly wish to speak with you on Sayn Wittgenstein's share in Liszt's litterary work. There's no denying she spilt milk for him. I found this out in Weimar from her and from her old friends. Isn't Fremstadt a stunning *Kundry?* How is Mrs. Finck? We both feel desperately in arrears with calls. But Mrs. Huneker's sister is just dead and naturally we are depressed. I'm reading proofs of a new volume. More bother!

Regards from house to house.

As ever

JIM HUNEKER.

Henry T. Finck.

To Henry T. Finck

(Confidential)

981 Madison Ave.
April 11, 1905

DEAR HARRY:

I really don't know what I have done to deserve all the pleasant reference you make to my work in the *Post*. And to think that I was in a Strauss storm-centre and didn't know it! That, however, is a meterological fact—the absolute centre of a cyclone is still. I had heard at Scribner's that someone had "kicked" over that footnote—certainly I had not; though please do not quote me as saying so. The whole thing is trifling. I was more annoyed at the conscienceless way a Mr. Ashton-Johnston rifled Niecks, Finck and myself for his detestable *pot-pourri* on Chopin. Certainly, the ethics of quotation have been overstepped—and the cockney abuses Niecks and myself into the bargain. What a joker! Have you read Adelhei v. Schorn's memoirs of Liszt and one Sayn-Wittgenstein? They are now in French as well as German. I called on her in 1903 at Weimar. Her memories are diverting. I am not mistaken when I believe—am I?—that Mr. Towse wrote the critical notice of "Iconoclasts" in the *Post* last Saturday. It was very fair, very sympathetic. Did you get the copy I sent you?—or was it only thunder I heard in the western heavens the other night? At first I mistook it for a Finckian snort of disapproval and I said: "Harry is reading the chapter on Maeterlinck!" Perhaps I flatter myself—you haven't looked at the "machine." The Liszt goes on apace. Scribner's wish me to keep it down to 125,000 words! How can I?

And, oh! the Paderewski recital! I was there. *He* sent me two seats—he never forgets his old friends. I also heard d'Albert play the Liszt H. moll sonata,—who *thumped* then! I didn't see you— If you weren't there you could have heard the great little man sitting in your office. I read your notice. I read your *Faust* symphony notice. I also, to my sorrow, read some of the others. *Incroyable!* And the notices of Paderewski's decadence! Christ in heaven can't they see that the man had to *grow* or else degenerate. Perry is right—and wrong. Paderewski does play differently, has been playing differently for the past five years. If he pounds occasionally—is it not, after all, Paderewski pounding? He is becoming a Rubenstein and Liszt rolled into one. I've eased myself in the *Metropolitan* of June (out May 15). To compare him with Joseffy is unjust. Paddy belongs to the impressionistic school —all color, vibration, tone. He paints by the *mass;* Joseffy by the line. And yet, Harry, I suspect Joseffy is the profounder artist of the two piano artists.

Accepts my thanks for your many encouraging
references to me—and my apologies for the infliction
of this letter—my nerves get rattled at such things.
I never cared for the operatic Paderewski—but as a
marvellous piano virtuoso—it is to scream!

As ever

Henry T. Finck.   JIM.

To Henry T. Finck

Rome, Oct. 9, 1905

DEAR HARRY:

The Fischer of this hotel, upon whose hideous note
paper I address you, formally kept the Hotel Alebert in *Vicolo* Alebert, where Liszt always sojourned
in Rome. We slept there one night. It is cheap,
mean. The former rooms of Liszt which com-
manded a noble view of the Pincian Gardens, no
longer exist—even the building is torn down. But
at Tivoli, at the Villa d'Este we were in his old
rooms, now the rooms of the Father Superior of
the Mariamte Monastery. Also at the St. Francesco
Kloster is a room of his. He is still vividly remembered after 20 years! And in Rome! We were
received by Leo X. in audience (300 other pilgrims)
and photographed with his Holiness—who recalls
Liszt with a loving memory. This pope is very
musical. Rome is not. I never heard such bad
church singing as here. Hope to see you on my re-

turn next month. Lots of Liszt *äna*. Regards from both to Mrs. Finck and your illustrious self.

As ever

Henry T. Finck. Jim.

To E. E. Ziegler

Dec. 3rd, 1905 (?)

DEAR NED:

Thanks for letter and invitation. *No* opera for us; besides, it won't be necessary to bother you, as I can get seats when I want them—which won't be until March. I know the *T. T.* voracity for seats. *Don't* give in too much. The Col. dear old Col. would take your socks with his bluff soldierly air, &c., &c. You know! Marty is a goner. Defoe says he has convulsions. Poor old fellow, and this is the end of the newspaper man—cruel as it seems, and is. We plough our skulls until the harvest refuses to appear—and then we go to a hospital. I have still, *Deo Gratius,* my fingers. I play every day. In my senility I may be able to teach piano, or—play something brisk and "lively" when the ladies get hold of a "gentleman friend" from Brooklyn who opens wine! Bordel, Bordelaise, Bordello, Borderland of insanity. Defoe says musical stuff is being ground out by a "young man from Oxford." Poor young man from Oxford! He gets in the first and last lines of long, elaborate notices—and weeps copiously in

the morning when he reads his castrated criticisms.
Poor young man! The *World* is famous for its slash-
ing night city editors. Marty was a sufferer; so is
Defoe. He assured me that as soon as the inevitable
had occurred he would consider your case. About
1,300, including Liebling and Klein are on the trail
of the job. Buzzards! Scavengers! Undertakers.
Keep blur to yourself—remember! Klein had a letter from J. F. R. *He* wishes to come over here, as
you are informed, but for some reason Klein is singu-
larly disturbed at the news. "Why the fellow drinks
a quart of Scotch every day," he remarked to us at
Daly's the other night. "Perhaps he wishes to change
his luck with Bourbon," I hazarded. What repartee!
Hell! The Missus wishes you up, but not until the
house is newly renovated, refurnished, &c. Then for
one jolly old time dinner—just the old trio. Busy!
My God! I've a contract with Russell. He is persistent. Five cents a word. Got money in advance,
&c. Begin January number *Metropolitan* with "Parsifal" story. It's a horror. Dramatic stuff in Jan.
Ainslee's, Materlinck's stories in Harper's *Bazar* and
the *Lamp* for January. Just finished careful Strauss
study—on new lines, absolutely—for *Scribner's*
March number. Busy! Must get back some of the
money I squandered last summer. The theatres are
doing nicely—thank you. If you get a chance at
Scribner's for December, Christmas Number, read

the "Master of Cobwebs." I'm getting even with that perennial humbug, the American Composer. The portrait, as you will note, is a composite. The idea is—well, at least novel. If critics stopped thinking of some composers, *i.e.*, stopped writing about them, where would they be? Voyez vous? Inky creations most of them.

As ever

Jim.

E. E. Ziegler.

To George Sylvester Viereck

981 Madison Ave.,
Monday morning,
Jan. 29, 1906

DEAR VIERECK:

Your notice was much too flattering; you gave a measure of praise full to overflowing—quite in accord with your generous, poetic nature. I return, herewith, the journal. I spoke to Moffat, Yard & Co., 289 Fourth Avenue (near 23rd St.) about those plays. It is a new, young, enterprising firm (formerly with Scribner's), and the two gentlemen wish to see your work. Will you call on them some morning or afternoon this week? They are very successful, and it may come to something. Make concessions in your copy. Life is a series of concessions— adaptations the biologists call them. "All or nothing" is lovely as a motto—in print; in life it leads to the gaol or madhouse. Pardon these truisms. It is Monday morning!

Sincerely with renewed thanks,

Yours,

JAMES HUNEKER.

George Sylvester Viereck.

To Henry T. Finck

The Carrollton, 981 Madison Ave.
January 30, 1906

DEAR HARRY:

I was glad to get your letter; surprised at the *Tageblatt* notice which I hadn't seen; and delighted at the d'Agoult clipping. I've had a dozen orders out for her *"Mes Souvenirs"* but the book is quite vanished. I would give a lot to get hold of her portrait—that, too, seems impossible. Have you ever seen one? Have you one? I'm sure her forehead and chin recede! Yes, Mrs. MacDowell told Mrs. Huneker that there is no hope. It's too horrible. I haven't been able to hear Miss Deyo play. This is a house of mourning. Mrs. Huneker's sister died last week, the second sister she has lost within a year. And this was her favorite, her companion, who with her husband accompanied us to Italy last summer. Altogether I've not had much time for pleasures— music is a luxury nowadays. I think, Harry, and I'm sure you will agree with me that the *Post* did not treat me fairly in that grotesque *Town Topics* trial. It dumped my name in with a lot of ruffians I never even heard of. I resigned from *T. T.* in 1902. I followed Schwab in 1897 and during the 5 years I wrote musical criticism for the journal I never indulged in personalities of my predecessors. All the more absurd and unfair was the pillorying of my name. There is nothing to be done now—to explain would be fatal; but I do think that, if in the future my name comes up again, it might be kept out of the *Post*, a journal for which I entertain a special reverence. I would tell the Editor this but —what's the use!

As ever

JIM.

Henry T. Finck.

To Henry T. Finck

981 Madison Ave., N. Y.
Feb. 15, 1906

DEAR HARRY:

Only a line to say that the *Metropolitan* people are sending you a copy of the March issue which contains a story of R. W. and Mathilda Wesendonck. The facts are not new to you, though they will be to the public. I have dug deeper than Kobbé in his *Herald* article. The point I make may interest you, as it is and has been your own for years: no one has any right to "kick" about Wagner's acceptance of money from his friends, least of all the people who helped him. And they did "blab," most of them, Liszt being the exception—as usual. In reading the proofs of my new book "Iconoclasts," the name of *Finck* bobbed up from the types, though the contents of the "agony" (in 435 p.) is totally dramatic. *You* are my King Charles head—— I can't keep you out of my books! At last, with my skirts clear of the last book I'm afloat in the Liszt. And now I no longer groan because I'm interested. The work has become fascinating and if Liszt lacks the *peculiar* genius of Chopin, he is so much bigger, broader as a man that the life of the one reminds me of a solitary pool at evening beneath melancholy willow-trees, while the other—a broad glittering plain, the sun shining bravely in the shack of glittering armies and the—well, you know what Liszt is: a musical cosmos; he contained all modern Artistic Tendencies even R. Strauss, emphatically his son, though an eccentric one. Jean Marnold in the *Mercure de France* has at last dealt a body blow to the pretensions of Berlioz. It makes fine reading, Berlioz, he says, is *not* a great maker of music, though a marvellous maker of sounds. Liszt, he declares, *thought* music as well as painted it. Best of all, Henry, a young man from the University of Strassburg has written a superb book on Bach the Romanticist, the Symbolist, the Poet and Painter. Your darling theories about Bach are incarnate in the book which is on its way to me from France. A preliminary article in a new Parisian review made me stare—at last Bach is placed in the right perspective, not as a manufacturer of dry as dust fugues but as a living man, writing programme-music and anticipating Liszt!!!! Won't H. E. K. weep? I must

halt. I'm invading the magazines and earning about
treble over my income on the daily newspaper, and
I have leisure! In the morning Joseffy technics,
and Bach and Liszt: afternoon walks and reading;
evening—writing. No theatres, no opera—silliest of
all dissipations, no concerts. Envy me! I fear I'll
die young(!) because the jealousy of the Gods. Pardon the loquacity. Regards from house to house.
Hope to see you soon.

As ever

Henry T. Finck.   JIM.

To Perriton Maxwell

981 Madison Ave.
April 8, 1906

DEAR MR. MAXWELL:
   Here is June dramatic "copy"—and two days ahead
of schedule! Hot stuff, too. I covered all the plays
except "Frenzied Finance," which I hear is beneath
contempt, critically. I also missed a vaudeville
"twin" by Edna Wallace Hopper, "Captain January"
at the Colonial; and I must plead guilty for not going to the Yorkville Theatre to see the Bimbergs
incidentally and "The Red Carnation" with Odette
Tyler before and behind—the curtain! Otherwise,
every show is touched upon. The Belasco letter with
which I head my story is valuable "copy." It may
start tongues to wagging again on a much disputed

theme. Can you rake up Paderewski and Joseffy
pictures? They would greatly enhance the story.
The two fought a long distance duel during the past
10 days and as I attended both concerts—hugely
patronized by the way—I wrote a few lines. I send
herewith a picture addressed to me at your office.
You can print it or keep it until next season—when
the Cyrus Townsend Brady play—isn't that the
name?—is to go on. Also a photograph of Vance
Thompson—one of the co-authors of "The Lady
Shore," deformed by his wife and others. I tell the
story in its entirety. If you want to use the Thompson head—monocle and all—save it for me. I'll
drop in soon and autograph that volume I sent you.
I hope you got it.

Salaam! As ever

JAMES HUNEKER.

May I expect proofs of copy?

To E. E. Ziegler

Thursday, Feb. 22nd, 1906

DEAR NED:
Thanks for clipping. I was reading Vambery's
History of Hungary yesterday so appreciate the clev-
erness of the pun—a Hunyadi did fight the Turks.

We go to Phila. late Saturday or early Sunday to stay over Monday. There is some business to be transacted, as the P. R. R. has bought a property of ours in Camden—that means signatures and notaries, &c. A bore, as millions are not involved. Yes, I was at the Empire Monday night to see Alf Hayman for tickets in re "The Duel." I also saw Eaton. But I was at home by 10 p. m., tucked away with the angels in my innocent couch. How are things?

As ever

JIM.

16th. Hungarian Rhapsody composed—Buda, 30th April, 1882; published 1882. Also a four hand arrangement. The first batch of Rhapsodies—No. 1 to No. 15 are his transpositions of Hungarian melodies best expressed; the last 5—from No. 16 to 19 (No. 20 is in MS.) all written after 1880, are more *nach Klange*, and nearly all four were composed for a special occasion. No. 16 was for the Buda-Pest Munkácsy celebration (M. is, as you know, the Hungarian painter); No. 18 for the Budapest Album of its exposition; No. 19 after a Czardaz of Abrányis.

But in all, despite their variegated ornamentation the *Hungarian scale* has been built upon. And this is all I know, the analysis of the composition I leave to you.

JIM.

E. E. Ziegler.

To E. E. Ziegler

Friday, June 8, 1906

You Dear Old Chump:

I hope you are by this time rid, well rid, of your crooked thoughts. Such suspicions are not worthy of you, Edward! Now Edward! I've been in the country with the Missus, down at John's ranch—not in Jersey, where he is building a bungalow in the Pines; but at Darlington, Del. Co. Pa. I've not been well; eyestrain from gout. Mrs. Huneker is not well: eyestrain from James—I suppose—and now I'm writing with both hands and feet to catch up. Ibsen will be a small silver mine for me—that's if dates and magazines don't clash. I purposed meeting Krehbiel before he went away. He gave me his itinerary, but he skipped a week earlier. I learned this from Tapper. Lots to tell you when we meet. Marsh is to meet me next Monday at Grand Union, 1 p. m. Can't you come up for luncheon? I hope you will. I didn't understand your allusion to Spanuth. Is he going to Berlin as a trip? And when? I hope he will not leave N. Y. for good. I'm sure he would tire of Germany in a year—I would. So would you. Did you get the Newman book? I left it on the desk downstairs at the Aeolian, E. 32nd St., two weeks ago, or more. You were not in. I saw many horses and some large "powerful uneducated persons" about.

How is Mrs. Ziegler, and how does Bright Eyes like the Country? It must be lovely. Of course we are both going down. Did you think you could escape us—said the City mice to the bucolic mice. Monday then.

As ever

JIM.

E. E. Ziegler.

To Perriton Maxwell

Tuesday, June 16, 1906

DEAR PERRITON:

Enclosed O.K. Your criticism of the "sheeny" anecdote is correct; only——

Used as I use it, it acquired a new and horrid significance. It was not put forward as a novelty— but to point a moral and adorn a tale. My mail this morning and yesterday contains at least 5 protests from my clerical brethren! *Entre-nous,* the story was hurriedly written—and entre-nous, the Hebraic prelude was, in my opinion, in bad taste. I spoke of this story to you and to Mr. Russell. I had promised it to Mr. J. I. C. Clarke. And Mr. Minor recalled to me that promise. There was no escape. Could I perhaps sell you another version—something quite novel; the pope could be red-headed and might curse the photographer. I wish he had. Thank you for sending those copies to various persons. The

New York end has acknowledged the reception. I've softened the Bernhardt tale.

Tout à vous

JAMES HUNEKER.

I've had, dear Maxwell, two (2) of those offers I spoke about. Dailies. But my heart is true to Poll! Note this and remind the marble-hearted publisher R. H. Russell that some day he may lose me. I suspect him plotting another downfall in rates? Thanks, also for sweet dab in re Shaw article. *Really* —Perriton!

To Mrs. Samuel W. Moore

Forest Hill Hotel,
Franconia, N. H.
Sept. 27, 1906

DEAR MRS. MOORE:

Your letter found me here evading my hay-fever. It is my first summer in America for many years; I had to write a series of impressionistic studies for Mr. Bennett; New York *Herald;* hence my stay here. I go to New York next week, and will go at once to Scribner's. I know about Elise Polko's work. There may be something in the scheme for Scribner's —and I hope for you. If not I have another firm in view. Thanks for the reference to my crabbed study

JAMES HUNEKER
From a photograph taken when a child

of Ibsen. But did you see the study in *Scribner's Magazine*, September? It was better and the pet of my old age,—my "Visionaries." Have you read it? It appeared last Fall (1905: *Scribner's*). Like the last book of all writers it seems the best. I'm glad you still remember me.

Sincerely, as ever,

JAMES HUNEKER.

I sail to Germany, Oct. 11, but will write before I go. I'm going especially to hear Richard Strauss's "Salomé," at Dresden; the score is colossal.

To W. B. Chase

The Carrollton,
981 Madison Ave.
Oct. 5, 1906

CHER MAÎTRE:

I thank you for the music—arrangements of Bach, veritable triumphs of transposition and taste. I am writing a life of Franz Liszt, and in it I shall not fail to speak of Isidor Philipp, who so happily carries on the work of arts the first great "arranger" for piano.

Je vous prie d'agréer l'expression de ma confraternelle amitié.

JAMES HUNEKER.

William Chase.

To David A. Munro

The Carrollton
981 Madison Avenue
Aug. 12, 1906

DEAR MR. MUNRO:

Here is the copy, relieved of 8 pages, 2,000 words.
The entire story was nearly 7,000 words; it is now
not more than 5,000. As I couldn't slaughter that
first part outright—it would make the study all tail
and no head—I made cuts in both sections; which
render the affair more symmetrical. I have re-folioed
the pages and think there are no breaks in the transi-
tions. If you wish to avoid the labor of proof reading I shall be only too glad to read the galleys myself.
My address until October after Tuesday next will
be in care of "Forest Hill" Hotel, Franconia, New
Hampshire.

I can return proofs within 24 hours after receiving
them. Again thanking you for your courtesy in this
matter,

I am Sincerely Yours,

JAMES HUNEKER.

David A. Munro.

And my dear Mr. Munro, chucking aside all editorial reserve, won't you, on my return, either take

luncheon or dinner with me! I know that the "contributor" is a "suspect"; but I know you so long and
I like you, personally, so much—you see I have the
Celtic courage—that I dare this risk, the risk of re-
fusal. Don't you remember the dinner you gave me
at that Italian place on Sixth Ave. opposite the car-
barns at 50th St.? I do! It must have been in 1886
—20 years ago. Don't say no! Particularly as my
vanity was slain at a stroke when I re-encountered
you at your office. I was a young fellow in 1886;
now I'm an old one; and you are exactly, why not
say precisely? the same Mr. Munro!

Let us meet in the autumn and then you may tell
your recipe for keeping young, though an editor!

J. H.

To David A. Munro

The Carrollton,
981 Madison Avenue
Dec. 11, 1906

DEAR MR. MUNRO:

As editors are always delighted to get an excuse
to rid their files of stale manuscripts permit me to
tell you that the death yesterday of Ferdinand Brunetière, the famous Parisian critic and editor of the
Revue des Deux Mondes, may furnish you with the
necessary excuse for printing that story of mine on

Anatole France, as the duel between France and Brunetière was, and is, notorious. I refer to it. And if this sounds in the nature of a joke, let the contributor have his little fun and forget all about the matter. How are you? I'm up to my eyebrows in work. *Entre nous* our friend Maurice, in Washington, must have his hands full running the Roman Catholic end of the complicated Roosevelt machinery!

Sincerely yours,

JAMES HUNEKER.

David A. Munro.

To E. W. Morse

The Carrollton
981 Madison Ave., N. Y.
Thursday, Nov. 15, 1906

DEAR MR. MORSE:

Thank you for your cordial letter. Remember I submitted the material to your judgment, frankly expecting you to say what you thought. Your criticism did not surprise me as I know the book—if published —would lack unity. On the other hand, I fancied it might be amusing, at least in the entertaining sense; *i.e.*, there is plenty of variety in it. I would have been in this week to see you, but that, after a Turkish bath last Saturday, I felt so brave, that I rode home on an open car. Results too depressing to my vanity to relate, except to acknowledge that my reckless days are over. I caught a damnable cold, and have been indoors ever since, nursing a stomachache, and trying to turn out a decent review of Mrs. Dargan's book for the *North American* (she has great gifts, by the way). The object of this apparent discursion, my dear Morse, is this: If I had gone in on the receipt of your letter, I could have better explained my haste in the publishing of these miscellaneous essays. As I told you, the suggestion came from a certain publishing firm on Union Square. There might be some little money in the scheme, not much, but some. So I had resolved to let you see the projected book (of course), and then make my request. Now that you have shattered my hopes—pardon the venerable image!—I will tell you what I think, and ask the favor anyhow. First: let the book rip! If Charles Scribner & Sons won't print it, no one else shall. That's settled. Second: I need a little money. So I fancied one book the more would pave the way if I asked for an advance. I'm trying to raise a sufficient sum so that I can do little else for the next six months but work on the Liszt book. That I mean to make as sound, as sober, and as careful a piece of critical work as I can turn out; something far in advance of my Chopin—which was too flowery; something far superior to my "Iconoclasts" which was fetchy and lacking in unity. The job is terrific. I

have enough material for 1,000 pages; and it is just
here I propose to curb my natural reckless and
explosive tendencies to giving too much, and saying
the overmuch. I need leisure. I can't go back into
daily journalism and finish that book—Liszt is now
become an Old Man of the Mountains to me; he
haunts me day and night. This long preamble simply
resolves itself into asking you to beg Mr. Scribner
to let me have $500 (five hundred) on my account
of possible future royalties. I find that I have been
receiving about $250 a year, and sometimes more
from the sale of five or six books. I am sure the
amount is not so formidable that it need worry you
—it will work itself off in a year anyhow; especially
as the Liszt is to be given to you in May, 1907. I
owe but a trifle to the house.

The main point is that by December 1st I will
need the money, and if you can see your way to
advance it, I promise that my thanks will not be so
elaborate, though quite as sincere as this very long
letter. With my passion for details, I have told you
all. Now don't disappoint me! I'm building a
good, and I think a saleable book, and "Promenades"
can go hang, until Liszt is done and over with; then
perhaps—it might be taken up again. I am going
away Saturday to my brother's new bungalow in the
heart of the pine region of Jersey. I'm not well, and
I think a few days in the open will put me in my old

form—barring open Madison Ave. cars. Pardon
the length of this, and try to put me through in the
matter. I shall be grateful—as I always am, for
your continued interest in my truly negligible work.

Sincerely

E. W. Morse.   JAMES HUNEKER.

< 1907 >

To David A. Munro

981 Madison Avenue
Jan. 16, 1907

DEAR MR. MUNRO:

Don't think me either churlish or forgetful for not personally acknowledging your courtesy in re "Anatole France." At its appearance I hesitated about writing you—which I should not have done—simply because of the childish feeling that you might think I was looking for the cheque. And now that the cheque has come perhaps—but this is all super-subtle sensibility. Frankly, I avow, I'm in your debt. You sandwiched me in one of the most brilliant numbers of the *North American*—which fact you are cognizant of, if you recall the comments and quotations on the subject (not my article). Let me ask a favor. I work seven nights a week; in the daytime I visit the picture galleries, send in copy by the gallon to the *Sun* (I went back to the *Sun* staff Dec. 1st) about the picture galleries and furnish 3 or 4 editorials a week. I give the Saturday *Times* a book review every fortnight. And I'm under contract with the *Herald* to supply a Sunday article monthly. I don't boast of this, Mr. Munro—a slave can't boast—but I tell you it to show how I'm crushed in at all sides for time. But—and I now am at the end of this interminable loop—I fight for my Saturdays. Hence I beg of you, as an old, old friend, to take luncheon with me some Saturday (after the next one) at some quiet and delectable hostelry where we can in peace drink a glass of good Burgundy (I say claret though it's not binding) and talk of the devil and all his works! Don't say no! You don't work on Saturday afternoon so come play with me as the classic Anna Held sings! There is downtown Mouquin's, upstairs where the wine is better than Delmonico's, where the place is deserted in the afternoon. And for fear your Scotch nose sniffs more *"copy"* let me assure you in advance that I haven't a scrap of an article for sale; nor would I take advantage of you if I had. I mention Mouquin's because it is near you, and I could fetch you there. Remember not a dinner with you unless you first lunch with me.

Cordially,

JAMES HUNEKER.

To David A. Munro

The Carrollton
981 Madison Avenue
March 4, 1907

MY DEAR MR. MUNRO:

Quite by accident at the Players Saturday, I met Mr. MacArthur and Mr. Forman, and then learned of your recent serious illness. I can't tell you how rejoiced I am to hear of your recovery; pneumonia is a subtle fiend. If you have looked at your mail,

how amused you must have been at my letter which
was sent when you were in the clutches of illness.
Luncheons and such are mockeries when we are on
our backs. But I do hope some time next month
when you are feeling yourself again you will give me
the pleasure of your company to luncheon, to dinner, in fact to anything from pitch and toss to man-
slaughter.

Sincerely yours,
James Huneker.

David A. Munro.

To David A. Munro

The Carrollton
981 Madison Avenue
May 13, 1907

My Dear Mr. Munro:

You were sadly missed at the little Jersey country
party yesterday my brother gathered. Poor Smyth
was toasted and your name was more than once on
our lips. My brother, John, told me that he had
heard from Smyth that I had perhaps offended you
in some way or other. I hope this is not so. I have
written to you 3 times, but received no answer. Did
you ever see those letters? I write now to ask you if
I may write a study (it is half done) of Joris-Karl
Huysmans for the *North American?* He died yesterday—Sunday—in Paris, and his qualities as a

man, critic, creator are so rare, so subtle, that he deserves a careful study in the *Review*. And if I mistake not he has never received one. He went over to Rome a few years ago and his "Lourdes" is wonderful. I am treating him not as a religious man as much as a literary—though the phenomena (or mechanism) of conversion I have not overlooked. There is no hurry about the story; only I should like exceedingly well to speak first for it—that is if you are contemplating one.

Sincerely, as ever,

David A. Munro.   JAMES HUNEKER.

To David A. Munro

The Carrollton
981 Madison Avenue
May 15, 1907

DEAR MR. MUNRO:

I'm a damned chump, and a cruel one! I might have known that you disliked writing and awaited a chance to tell me when I called what I wanted to know. And I was about to call but I'm in an Inferno of pain for the last week—an abscess of the upper jaw (I suppose a penance imposed upon me by the Almighty because I chatter so much on paper. I write reams of letters every week). I'll do the Huysmans the next few weeks and keep it to 5,000 words. I'll do my level best too: I like to figure in the *Review*. The crowd

was a bit glowing on Sat. night but rum works wonders. A furious discussion set in after I remarked
that Raphael's Madonnas were inferior to Eugene
Carrier's. What with beer and æsthetics we spun the
night out till 2:30. Sunday was a glorious day.
Next autumn you must go down. I'll pick the crowd.
Few but fit. Thanks for the dinner invitation. I'll
try as soon as my face ceases aching.

Sincerely,
JAMES HUNEKER.

David A. Munro.

P. S. Dr. E. J. Nolan, librarian of the Philadelphia Academy of Natural Sciences and a warm friend
of Egan's, was in the party. He represented the
Church Militant!

To David A. Munro

981 Madison Avenue
July 3, 1907

MY DEAR MR. MUNRO:

Here is the Huysmans story, as complete as I could
make it within the 5,000 word limits. It may be less
than 5,000; it is not any more. I had expected to
give it to you 6 weeks ago but since then I've been
almost living at the Hahnemann Hospital where Mrs.
Huneker hovered between life and death for weeks.
I hope you will like the study; I've taken pains and

as I have been a reader of Huysmans for 20 years I fancy details are right. As to his conversion I neither doubt nor praise it—a dispassionate attitude is the safest; besides the sincerity of the unhappy man is not to be impugned. His deathbed was something too horrible to pin to paper. May I see the galley proofs? Also, let me apologize for not accepting your kind invitation to the club; but I've been through the valley of desolation these past weeks. I'm only thankful to say that matters might have been worse.

Sincerely your friend,

David A. Munro.   JAMES HUNEKER.

P. S.   Might I suggest in the event of your liking the article, that (hyphenated) "J.-K. Huysmans" be the title for the cover—the regular article I have prepared by—what I think is a better title.

To David A. Munro

981 Madison Avenue
July 11, 1907

DEAR MR. MUNRO:

Your kind invitation came when I was downtown shooting at an editor who believes in Christian Socialism. I tried after my return to get you on two phones, but in vain. At the Players they sent another Mr. *Munroe* (presumably) to the receiver. However, it would have been impossible for me to

accept the—welcome—bidding to dinner. I am now
a nurse, a garde-malade, and, while I occasionally
get away for a few hours in the afternoon, it is not
easy to leave my convalescing wife alone—save the
uncertain custody of a sleepy servant. But later—
later! I hope to make up for my last thirst—about
the only spirit I have, which, when summoned from
the vasty deep, inevitably comes at my bidding
(Percy vs. Glendower). I may add that I am sorry,
very sorry. Apropos of nothing in this note, did the
story of Huysmans the saint reach you? I hope it
may please.   Sincerely,

                                    JAMES HUNEKER.

D. A. Munro.

To Charles J. Rosebault

                                The Carrollton
                            981 Madison Ave., N. Y.
                                Feb. 28, 1907

DEAR KARL:

I gasped! But what has such a little thing as a
newspaper to do with an important luncheon engagement? Name your weapons—that is the place and
hour and let it be Saturday (unless you have another
engagement). I'm damned sorry all the same. The
Sun will miss you. I know I shall. You've proved
a mighty good comrade to me and while I hate gush
I wish to thank you now for all the sympathy you've

shown in the past. I'll say kaddish for you—although it is rather an informal way of expressing gratitude, particularly as you are not my father!

I'll go down early to catch the chief and will meet you at 1, or 1.30—anywhere—Savoy, 59th st., or at the Players. (Only I don't want to get loaded—I have an engagement at 6.30 with my dearest foe, Mrs. Huneker.) So drop me a line here by Friday night—I go seldom downtown now—heavens knows I went little enough before, but I'll reach the vanishing point for whom will I see in your office! What new Ghost! Some stern browed bastard who will cut my column rates.

Regards as ever,

JIM.

P. S. Dithmar tells me Mrs. Rosebault has returned. I hope she is feeling better. Our regards. (And we must have that night here, this Spring sure!)

Charles J. Rosebault.

To Mrs. Samuel W. Moore

The Carrollton
981 Madison Avenue, New York City
Mar. 14, 1907

MY DEAR MRS. MOORE:

I was exceedingly mortified when I received your letter this morning, not because I felt that I had been remiss because the last publishing house to which I

submitted your manuscript had promised me to write
you—I gave them your address. First I tried Scribner's who, after some debating, concluded they could
not touch the book on account of its having been
written so long ago. Then I tried another firm,
which disposed of the case at once—couldn't touch
musical novels. Finally, I submitted your scenario
to Moffat, Yard & Co., where it still is. They are a
young firm, formerly with Scribner's, and Robert S.
Yard listened with interest to the scheme. On my
return from Europe he still held the matter under
advisement. A month or so I again asked him.
He replied that he feared, &c. Then said, "I'll write
Mrs. Moore and say why." He said he would. And,
of course, he didn't. I advise you, my dear lady, to
drop him a line—Mr. Robert S. Yard, Moffat, Yard &
Co., East 17th st., Union Square, New York City—
and ask if there is any hope of acceptance. In the
interim I'll prod his memory. I regret the con-
tretemps, but it is really not my fault. Yes, I saw
"Salomé," twice in Germany, 5 times in New York,
of which 2 were full dress rehearsals. It is easily the
greatest score since "Tristan and Isolde"; even the
emotional intensity of Wagner has been surpassed—
in Salomé's final song. Furthermore it follows the
book with miraculous exactitude, follows, yet inter-
prets. It is the beginning of a new art—rather that
fusion of the arts dreamed of by Wagner, though
never realized by him—except in wonderful mo-

ments—because his musical temperament over-mastered him and drove drama to a subordinate position. As to the disagreeable, morbid part of the affair, don't believe a word of what you read. The work was withdrawn for political reasons, not artistic. It is not nearly so offensive, lewd and suggestive as "Carmen"—as Calvé's Carmen (was femaley). So you can see it was not so bad; above all, it is not vulgar. The head, gruesome as it is, is like any death's head when placed on the stage. Isolde sings passionately over Tristan—who is dead though his head is not severed from his body. No, the public will see "Salomé" next season as it is seeing Bernard Shaw's very moral "Mrs. Warren's Profession" this week in the city—and it will then wonder what all the pother was about. Politics *i.e.*, the hatred for certain directors of the opera—Morals! in vulgar New York, with the vile Thaw Trial, its vulgar theatres! In the *Bookman* of March I have a few lines on "Salomé." The story is stale hence I can't write about it for the magazines—it would be too stale by publication time. I'm working on new Frenchmen, Anatole France (published *North American Review,* Jan. 4) and now on Maurice Barrés for the *Atlantic;* also doing art criticism this winter for the *Sun.* I'm very busy. Pardon long letter.

As ever,

JAMES HUNEKER.

Mrs. Samuel Woodward Moore.

To George Sylvester Viereck

The Carrollton
981 Madison Avenue
May 22, 1907

MY DEAR VIERECK:

You will pardon me for not having acknowledged your poems when you hear that I've been ill for 2 weeks—not a line have I written until today for the *Sun* or letters. A bad dental abscess has tormented me for ten days. It's better now. Last night late I at last ventured to read your verse. I knew most of it from the German. It goes very well in English. It's a milestone, my boy; you'll look back at it some day and wonder. The preface is a mistake. You will find that out, too, at no distant time. In reality you are modest, even timid in your innermost nature. Why then the pose of vanity? You do not need to boast your verse—it is good and you are gifted. But why tell the world! Leave that sort of thing to the Shaws and the Wildes—who are not, were not real poets.   As ever,

J. H.

To E. P. Mitchell

The Carrollton
981 Madison Ave.
May 24, 1907

DEAR MR. MITCHELL:

Thank you for your sympathetic letter. I don't deserve sympathy because at the end of 10 days an

old negro woman told me that I was a fool to suffer—
a hot fig would "draw the cess!" The dentist didn't
know this, no more I. What jokes men are! I
was preparing a Huysmans story for the *N. A. Review*
when I read with interest and amazement your extraordinary idea of the Pain Epicures. Why did you
not include it in a volume? Huysmans would have
mixed up the idea with sadistic and lubricous imagin-
ing; but to you belongs the priority in a field the unhappy (neuralgic) Frenchman made his own. The
truth is the scale of pain and pleasure tones often
meet; pain may be the complementary tone of
pleasure. I'll send down that impressionistic story
later. I've had a private peep at the new Renoir at
the Museum. I first saw it in 1879, Paris.

Sincerely, my dear Mr. Mitchell,

JAMES HUNEKER.

E. P. Mitchell.

To E. P. Mitchell

The Carrollton
981 Madison Ave.
May 30, 1907

DEAR MR. MITCHELL:
The idea of writing a little story of impressionism
for the *Sun* (and for the layman who loves art) has
worried me all winter. The result of that worriment

is enclosed; pray do not be alarmed at its profuse-ness—I have broken the story into 2 parts; the first deals with the new Renoir canvas at the Museum ($18,000 picture); part second relates of Renoir and Impressionism. I have endeavored—by the aid of available quotations—to answer that puzzling question:—What is Impressionism? On the technical side I allowed M. Mauclair to answer; but I've drawn very liberal conclusions on my side. If the procedure of the *Sun* permits I think the story as far as page 7 might go into one issue; the balance the day following. Sunday—Monday? (with the same title). However, that is for you to say. There are about 4,000 words—too many, I fancy, for a single issue—when I see you sometime next month,—I hope—Mr. Mitchell, I will relate to you the Higher Egoism (a la Max Stirner) crumbled in the presence of another's suffering. I fear I am not a Pain Epicure just now.

Sincerely,

JAMES HUNEKER.

E. P. Mitchell.

To George Sylvester Viereck

Thursday (1907?)

DEAR VIERECK:

Thank you for your kind inquiries about Mrs. Huneker. She is out of danger and will leave the hospital soon I hope. I shall do little more this summer now—health is better than art, any day in the week. And health we must seek. The *Century* story is a bit of foolery; in the *Bookman* for July there is a better (psychologically considered) story— the *Smart Set* story, "Posthumous," is founded on fact. Madame Michelet printed volume after volume although her husband had died—and she signed his name to them all; posthumous works! Some say it is the case with the Sharps (Fiona Macleod). Anyhow *you* will see the point; the public only the faded sentiment. It may interest you to know that the *Atlantic* in the August or September number prints a study on Maurice Barrés, the *North American Review* one on Huysmans, and the *Scribner's*—next Fall—an elaborate study of Henry Stendhal-Beyle —all written this Spring before Mrs. Huneker's illness. Since then I've done nothing. Life is drab today.

I see your book is getting praised, abused, etc. But *always* noticed. And that's the chief thing. Silence alone is deadly criticism. When you write you set people's tongues going, people's pens toiling. Keep it up. I'll be glad to see that novel—about the life you haven't lived, as yet.

Sincerely,

JAMES HUNEKER.

George S. Viereck.

To E. P. Mitchell

The Carrollton
981 Madison Ave.
Aug. 16, 1907

DEAR MR. MITCHELL:

Enclosed stuff I had intended to write after Huysmans's death, May 12, but could not find the leisure.
It demanded much patience to go through his books
again, for I have written an elaborate study of him
as a literary artist for the *North American Review*
(not yet published). I hope you will like it and I
hope also that you liked that Phila. story. I looked
at the Sturgis booklet and was amazed at that plate.
Of course it is Piranesian in its exaggerations. And
my anxiety about Piranesi last week drove from my
memory the inevitable bother—for you—of my con-
tributions to the *Sun*. I mean that I forgot to send
you an account of the Saint Gaudens's editorial which
appeared Aug 4. Since then there has appeared only
the Piranesi (Aug. 11th), both articles in their entirety being a few inches over 3 columns. I wish to
tell you that the editorial leader in this morning's
Sun, "Absolutely Unbroken," is the most powerful,
because of its subtle simplicity, that has appeared in
years. The close so skillfully led up to recalls—
for me—one of Wendell Phillips's deadly, biting in-
terrogatories at the end of his most polished sarcastic

and glacial addresses.   Some one is to be congratu-
lated on the *Sun* in the use of the rapier.

Sincerely,

JAMES HUNEKER.

E. P. Mitchell.

To E. P. Mitchell

The Carrollton
981 Madison Ave.
Aug. 28, 1907

DEAR MR. MITCHELL:

The Symons book is new.   It is worth 2 cols.   The
Herald last Sunday gave it the greater part of a page
(art supplement).   Symons is an admirable writer
on art.   I wrote him for the book; he answered me
only last Monday that he had told the publishers to
send it to me.   So it all falls in right.   Of course
I'll review it—Blake is a great misunderstood genius.
I had Swinburne's "William Blake" & the Gilchrist
"Life."   If you will be so good to mail the Symons
to The Windsor, Cape May, N. J., I shall read it
leisurely and as soon as the sniffles cease, I'll write
something.   Thanks for your interest.

Sincerely,

JAMES HUNEKER.

E. P. Mitchell.

To George Sylvester Viereck

The Carrollton
981 Madison Ave.
Nov. 19, 1907

MY DEAR VIERECK:

You are very kind to invite me to the Prof. Burgess celebration.   I'm sorry I can't go, sorry I can't spend a pleasant evening near you and Prof. Munsterberg (of whom they sing in Boston: "Ein fested Gott ist Munsterberg!")   Won't you grüss the great man for me like a good fellow?   But I'm engaged and to the desk upon which I'm writing this—no more outings for me until August.

I'm only 6 months behind in my work, thanks to Mrs. Huneker's illness.   The verse you enclosed is music, but uncanny, as is all your recent work. "The Vampire" is uncanny—more so than the story first told by Byron's friend and physician.   Was ist los mit dir?   You must come down to earth.   Read Goethe, Goethe, Goethe!   He is the cure-all for soul sickness.

Cordially,

JAMES HUNEKER.

George Sylvester Viereck.

To E. E. Ziegler

The Carrollton
981 Madison Ave., N. Y.
Dec. 3rd, 1907

DEAR NED:

Was ist dir los? Was noch? I fancied you too
busy to see anyone. Of course I'm not "angry" or
"disgusted" and as for streaking off yesterday, I
had planned writing you to beg your pardon for hold-
ing you up at a street corner to ask a lot of questions.
And its news to me about the M. C. Endlich! You
are now somebody. I told you the *Herald* would
focus more fire on your work in a day than would
the *World* in a year—I did contemplate asking for
Pachman seats. He is quite crazy, but in these times
of piano banging and horrid pianola (observe that I
am brushing up my Italian!) his touch is a consolation. Again I feared to bother you. I have been
much in Phila. during the past 2 months. You see
as a man approaches the fifties he goes back to his
family. I am no exception. I am very domestic—
enfin. But I am no "hermit." I go out daily. It
is simply because in N. Y. as in London (though not
the case in Paris or Berlin) when a man leaves one
current for another the currents are like parallel
lines—they never converge. I see a very important
world in art; never do I lay eyes on musical people,
not even Mrs. Ditson, which proves your old conten-

tion that N. Y. is more cosmopolitan than Paris: *i. e.*
no one pays any attention to another's affairs. However, all this is not answering your question. Certainly I'll lunch with you. Friday last I went to the
Gilsey but I fancy you went early to the Philharmonic.
I'm free Saturday, or Monday. Either day will do.
Name place, hour, &c. I'm only stipulating that we
do not eat where musicians or critics, or newspaper
folk do congregate. I'll meet you say at the Savoy,
or better still the middle room (42nd. street side of
the Grand Union; not the Flemish Café). I really
didn't think you were in a hurry to see me when you
wrote months ago. H. E. K. wrote a lovely little note
today and in answering it I spoke of your "hermit"
allusion defending myself. I go everywhere, even
to church, but not to the opera or that dull old Carnegie Hall. Why therefore do you conclude that I
am a hermit? Mr. Morgan doesn't think so; there,
now will you be good!

How is Mrs. Suzanne and the girlie? We often
speak of them. I'm up to my eyes in work. One
column a day on the *M. C.!* Is it work or play? And
money—phew! None in sight. I'm buying pictures—if I had the price, but I haven't. Enclosed is
hot shot. Save the *Courier* until we meet and write
soon.   As ever,

JIM.

With regards to the girls at home.

< 1908 >

From an old tin-type

JAMES HUNEKER

When a very young man

To E. P. Mitchell

The Carrollton
981 Madison Ave.
Feb. 1, 1908

DEAR MR. MITCHELL:

The coming week will be one of the heaviest of the season. To cover it adequately I have resolved to send down not more than a column or a trifle at a time. That may facilitate its getting into print easier. For the Sunday story—that is if I get a chance at Sunday—I shall reserve the criticism of the "Eight Painters" at Macbeth's. As it will not be a very long or an esoteric story I'll send it down by Thursday. I'll write it clearly and not need proofs. Enclosed was a labor of love—You with your fond‑ness for Spain and Spanish art will revel when you will tear yourself away from that terrible Editorial desk, and take a trip up the subway, Broadway divi‑sion, to 157th St., there alighting and going one block back to the new Hispanic Museum. What riches! What pictures—few but fit! No one in town has written an adequate story. The enclosed is certainly not, but at least it is not so full of misinformation as the story penned by the luckless *Times* man, that tall Scandinavian, Lauvrik, whose knuckles were rapped by Mr. Lathrop in the *Sun,* on the editorial page, the other week.   Sincerely,

JAMES HUNEKER.

P. S.   I don't think it will be necessary for me to
cover the Architectural League Exhibition after that
elaborate story on the front page of the *Sun* this
morning; part of it was a necessary news story, the
rest criticism.   J. H.

E. P. Mitchell.

To Dr. T. C. Williams

> The Carrollton
> 981 Madison Ave.
> April 2, 1908

DEAR TOM:
  I'm glad you read or dipped into "Visionaries,"
as duly reported by my spouse. The book was the
scrapings of my magazine articles for the past 10
years. It does not hang together—what volume of
short stories does! I'm writing Scribner's to send you
my "Chopin" and "Iconoclasts." Perhaps you may
remark the fact that the first—since translated into
German and French—is a real book, not a compila-
tion, and demanded for its execution years of con-
centrated effort. It is now the standard work for
teachers, so I am assured.
  The study of Ibsen—oh joyful whiskers—was, up
to the time of his death, the longest in the English
tongue (168 pages). Both these books will be of
value to you in your practice, being warranted to

cure, or alleviate insomnia, piles or the pip. I am
going to write that novel; but two other books are on
the bridge ahead of it; my Liszt life and a volume of
literary essays (due in 1909).

      Yours with brittle veins,

                As ever,

Dr. T. C. Williams.   JIM.

To Benjamin De Casseres

              The Carrollton
          981 Madison Avenue
            Aug. 2nd, 1908

DEAR CASSERES OF THE HOUSE OF BENJAMIN:

Of course I knew the handwriting on the paper
wall, and even if I hadn't the style would have be-
trayed you. The principal thing you suggested was
the question; perhaps others took that foolish Schopenhauerian tag of mine literally! I immediately wrote
and asked. If so I shall be more explicit in a foot-
note. The anecdote is a classic. To it Ashton Ellis
has devoted a chapter. Schopenhauer was shocked
at the incestuous finale to the 1st act of "Valkyrie."
Hence his prudish (and humorous) "High Time!"
Other comments he made on the "Ring" such as "second rate poetry," or "this fellow is a damned ass."
Furthermore, after hearing "Flying Dutchman" he
said that R. W. was not musical!! Schopenhauer pre-

ferred Rossini, and every afternoon when his nap was
over he tootled an hour on his flute. Rossini, flute—
Jessas! (The "Ring," by the way, has been cut often).
There is already a superb work on "Ennui" by Tar-
dieu, and its relations to art, with a study of Flaubert,
&c. The French got ahead of every one. Yes, I
read the 1st and 2nd versions (1849-1856) of Flaubert's "Temptation" in the *Revue de Paris*. Better
still, I saw the original MS. 20 years ago at Madame
Caroline Commain Villa (now Madame Franklin
Grout). I once saw Flaubert. He was tall, rubicund,
wore a red tie! His face was red, too, and heavily
lined. He walked ponderously (it was in 1879). He
was taking a short cut from the Grand Boulevard
through the Chausée d'Antin to the Boulevard Hauss-
mann, evidently making for the Gare Saint-Lazare.
Some one said: "Flaubert," I turned and stared. His
eye, a big moon swimming in a lake of sympathetic
liquid, blood streaked, turned on me. It was an opti-
cal shock. I was 19, wore long hair and a Scotch cap
(hell!) and he smiled! It was angelic in its indul-
gence. He recognized the idiot in me and was like a
God in this recognition. "Bouvard et Pécuchet" he
was working on at that time. He passed, his iron
gray hair falling on those vast shoulders—the world
had bowed them with its weight of inanities—and he
passed from my view. All day I walked around the
Batignolles saying: "I have seen Flaubert!" Even
knowing old Walt Whitman in Camden and escorting

him several times to symphony concerts at the Broad
St. Academy of Music, Phila.; even shaking hands
with Browning, or having seen Swinburne on the
British Channel, and, once, Victor Hugo, a cotton
umbrella in hand mounting the *impériale* of an omni-
bus opposite the Gáre du Nord, Paris; even these and
other encounters with men of genius have not left such
an impression as the sight of the solitary Flaubert,
poor, with but few old friends left, on his way to
Croisset near Rouen, there to take up the thread of
his work, his Book of Revenge, the most bitter book
ever penned by mortal, "Bouvard et Pécuchet" (all
the more bitter because its irony is so blithe). But
don't, my dear Casseres, let your philosophic gall
poison your blood. Hate, but hate as hates Anatole
France, not as Nietzsche (did you see that little story
of mine in the *Bookman*, in 1907, called "Mine
Enemy"? It deals with hatred as mainspring of am-
bition). Wear the Epicurean badge of smiling,
tolerant contempt for the foolish. Pessimism à la
Schopenhauer is all right; his successors are too bitter. Believe me, it is the bravest, gayest philosophy,
this Epicureanism. It is moderate; it smiles at the
inutile and fatuous and is only contemptuous of
one thing—the man without a *sense of humor*; *i. e.*
relatively proportion! In the relativity of things lies
the secret of personal salvation. Yours is not a tepid
soul; hence my allusion. I am old and tired of all-
personal salvation. My new book (1909) will con-

tain this *not* very novel doctrine, which befits my 48½
years and my increasing guts. (Fat is fatal.)

Yours, not without thirst,

J. H.

(If I add that I seldom write long letters it will
seem like paying myself a compliment. Don't write
me for a long time; I shan't have the time to answer.)
(Confidential, particularly the Flaubert episode—
which I shall use some day.)

Benjamin De Casseres.

To E. P. Mitchell

The Carrollton
981 Madison Ave.
Aug. 14, 1908

Dear Mr. Mitchell:

My sole contribution to the *Sun* during the past
week was:—"What Is Pragmatism!"

I was glad to see the above article in type—though
it is hardly light summer reading!—but gladder still
to get proofs of the "New York Cosmopolis" story.
I had feared its persistent optimistic tone. According to the *Evening Post,* also the *Century* people, our
tall towers are hideously ugly excrescences. I know
you don't see them that way; nor do I. The only way
to solve the problem is to make these "excrescences"

as beautiful as possible, and that is what some build-
ers are doing. They have come to stay, the tall towers
and marble battlements, and I'm very proud you
permit me to say these things in the *Sun*.

Sincerely,
JAMES HUNEKER.

E. P. Mitchell.

To Charles J. Rosebault

The Carrollton
981 Madison Ave.
Nov. 27, 1908

DEAR CHARLES:

Thanks for the picture. I had seen a reproduction
but nothing so satisfactory as this. I'll hang it where
I can see it often. Enclosed letter to Lorimer, also
card to send in with yours. He is a fine chap, Lorimer. Arch St., near 6th, is, I think, the address.
Hope to see you next month. I'm smeared with glue,
black with ink; on my lips are blasphemies—I never
knew until I re-read my old copy how rotten it was—
is. I'm building a book! God help the house!
Mrs. H. is out all day in despair. Talk about ob-
stetrics and births, &c., when a man gives birth to a
book it is the mountain in labor with a mouse (and
such a little mouse). Regards,

JIM.

Charles J. Rosebault.

To Charles J. Rosebault

Monday, 1908

DEAR CHARLES:

Here are "Ghosts" tickets. Don't miss the chance
—it is the last week and if you don't go there won't
be more than 9 or 10 people in the house!

But the play! Prepare to drink hard after it ends
—I should suggest Brandy with a dash of vitriol
mixed with a pint of absinthe; the whole taken at
a gulp.

Then perhaps you will sleep!

Sincerely as ever,

JIM.

Charles J. Rosebault.

< 1909 >

To Mrs. Rollins H. Wilbur

The Carrollton
Madison Ave., Cor. 76th St.
Jan. 18, 1909

MY DEAR MRS. WILBUR:

I'm very glad to know that you are better and at home. I reproached myself for sending you that morbid little study of a morbid sufferer—Nietzsche. Yet the Chopin suggested itself in this way. During the summer of 1907 Mrs. Huneker after a murderous operation rested "at home" at the Hahnemann Hospital, instead of a long contemplated trip to Spain! As I couldn't sit still long enough to write, being nervous and worried, I forced myself to get up this little Chopin collection—my favorite works, which I study and play almost daily. Ditson's had brought out an earlier volume, a collection of the popular music, the more banal Chopin. So they endured my choice of all the difficult larger compositions with my own cranky notions of phrasing and fingering. You will find some nasty fingering and perhaps some unusual accentuation. I get it all from my venerable master, Georges Mathias, a genuine pupil of Chopin. "So Chopin did it," he often said, when showing me some perilous passagework.

I will, however, always think of the hospital when I look at certain of these selections. It was a trying summer for both of us; a suffering, uncomplaining woman and a restless selfish man.

And you were at Brown's Mills in the Pines. I go there often. It is charming. The swimming in summer is excellent. My brother, John Huneker of Phila., has built himself a bungalow not far from the hotel, directly on the lake, "Huneker's Lane." He named the place "Huneker's Quest." It is pretty. A stag crowd usually invades of Sundays. Otherwise he lives at a glorious spot in Darlington, Del. Co. The Dohan Estate (he married one of the Miss Dohans). How odd you should have been in that New Jersey paradise. I never found it dull, especially as my brother has, for sport's sake, a duck and chicken farm about a mile away. I love chickens now more than I do Chopin, not to eat but to watch. The human variety of chickens, geese and ducks I get too much of here in crowded New York. Next Sat. *Scribner's* monthly for February will print a little study of mine on Charles Baudelaire, and next March, a new volume of essays, to me of far more interest than the iconoclastic group. Stendhal, Baudelaire, Flaubert, Anatole France, Nietzsche, Maurice Barrés, Max Stirner and several Mystics.

And now pardon my runaway pen. Pray don't answer this for letter writing will only fatigue your nerves. I think until you get stronger Bunyan's "Pilgrim's Progress," "Imitation of Christ"—both

noble books—will be more beneficial to your spirits
than the modern revolutionary image smashers.

I am very sincerely,

JAMES HUNEKER.

Mrs. Rollins H. Wilbur.

To Mrs. Charles H. Ditson

The Carrollton
981 Madison Ave.
Feb. 18, 1909

DEAR MRS. DITSON:

Of course you've forgotten all about that luncheon;
but I have not.   I write to beg you to defer it until
after the first week of April.   My book (pauvre
enfant!) is delayed; I'm reading proofs furiously;
and I'm trying to keep abreast of my daily labor.
Now you won't mind!   I enclose title; the sub-title is
to be: "A Book of Supermen."   The *Stendhal* study
will occupy 65 pages, the largest thus far in English.
I hope Mrs. Ditson will like the book.   It is full of
her favorite Frenchmen.   If *she* (who must be
obeyed!) likes it then the future of "Egoists" is assured.   Aren't the Sorrollos ripping fine.

Mrs. Huneker asks to be remembered.

Sincerely as ever,

JAMES HUNEKER.

Mrs. Charles H. Ditson.

To E. P. Mitchell

> The Carrollton
> 981 Madison Ave.
> Mar. 27, 1909

DEAR MR. MITCHELL:

I am giving myself the pleasure of sending you a personal copy of my new volume of essays, "Egoists," through the Scribners, sometime next month. They tell me a copy for review has been sent to Mr. Hazeltine, but I don't know whether he is well enough, or whether he would care to review a book of such character. It is not polemical, though the undercurrent toward individualism as opposed to socialism and communism is unmistakable. But there is a mass of biographical facts and some of the men dealt with are new, Max Stirner, Barrés, &c. Naturally, I would deem it an honor to be reviewed on Mr. Hazeltine's page but I wouldn't for the world ask him. If you will find leisure in the midst of your unceasing editorial whirl to glance occasionally at some of the essays I'll be very happy. The original *Stendhal* in *Scribner's Magazine* has been built up to 65 pages; some of the material will be familiar to you.

Sincerely as ever,

JAMES HUNEKER.

Edward P. Mitchell.

To Mrs. Samuel W. Moore

The Carrollton, 981 Madison Ave.
New York City
April 28, 1909

DEAR MRS. MOORE:

Your letter and splendid critique touched me much.
If I ever see George (and I haven't seen him for 10
years), I'll proudly display that notice of my little
book (which by the way I need hardly tell you is a
slight study of philosophic Egoism, for individualism
as expressed by a certain group with the men and
their pernicious teachings I have nothing in sympathy. I endeavored to be objective). It's strange
you, too, saw the Wickersham study. So did George,
who wrote at once a cordial charming note. If I
had had your data before I wrote it. I really put the
thing into print so as to stop the idiotic rumors floating about George's ancestry. Nothing derogatory,
au contraire. Not enough credit was given to George's
own individual achievement. But he had a good send-
off, didn't he? And I was determined that you and
your father would be credited, for their help in form-
ing his character. Uncle George Wickersham sees
my brother, John Huneker, at the Art Club in Phila.
He says he is 80 years old, which figure seems in-
creditable to me. Young Carl Gaertner, the cellist,
is dead, my brother wrote me yesterday. Louis
I never see. I'm glad you told me of the Walt

Whitman matter. But I never went on his (your) tickets. My share was confined to convoying the old bard to the nearest street car. The reason, my dear Aunt Aubertine, that I didn't include Carl Gaertner among the mighty was because he was in no sense a solo artist. He always played out of tune and he began to study his instrument too late to master its mechanism. But he had the feu sacrée.

Regards, as ever,
JAMES HUNEKER.

I enclose a clipping of my study of G. W.

To E. P. Mitchell

The Carrollton
981 Madison Ave.
April 28, 1909

DEAR MR. MITCHELL:

I have written Mr. Hazeltine, of course (and I've never had the pleasure of meeting him, though he knew my mother very well), but I must thank you primarily for the charming and adequate notice of that little book of mine in the Sunday *Sun*. I feel that without your initiative I might not have had the opportunity. I shan't forget your kindness. Curiously enough I received a letter from your old friend, W. W. Hensel, of Lancaster, Pa., who turns out to be an old friend of my brother John, of the Art Club,

Philadelphia. It appears that your name is circled by a halo at that club with Mr. Hensel and others.

Sincerely, as ever,

JAMES HUNEKER.

Edward P. Mitchell.

To E. P. Mitchell

The Carrollton
981 Madison Ave., N. Y.
May 6, 1909

DEAR MR. MITCHELL:

Thanks for the opportunity to read and review those letters; I may have slightly exceeded my allotted 1½ cols. I hope not. The theme is as fresh as ever and throws up an enormous amount of suggestions. I have been frank in piercing the Bayreuth bubble— i. e. the constant greed for money and the publication of the most sacred letters. Enclosed, also, that letter from "John Burroughs" (not *the* John, I presume), which, if you see fit to print, I haven't the slightest objection. It rather goes for several heads; and that makes interesting reading; though it is also a puff for Max Weber.

Sincerely, as ever,

JAMES HUNEKER.

E. P. Mitchell.

P. S. Sometime when I am in your office I shall ask you the etiquette of book reviewers in keeping or sending back books sent them for review. I simply do not know what is customary in such a case. The "Velasquez" of Bernetti I bought for my own use; but I still have the little primer of Bode and the Flemish-Dutch Masters. Also a dry as dust study in musical form. And this Wagner correspondence; if you may remember I returned Waldstein's book on "Herculaneum" as it is a valuable reference volume for your library.

To George Sylvester Viereck

The Carrollton
981 Madison Ave.
May 31, 1909

DEAR VIERECK:

Thanks for your labor of love, which I shall look forward to as an oasis in the sandy days of July. I am not well. Simply bored to death by books and art and New York. When I read yesterday that your father was in Deutschland I envied him. I have no photograph, not even one taken in 1900. The one the Scribners have was a pretty poor affair, taken in Weimar 2 years ago. But I'll sit and send you one anyhow. I dislike the camera. The reason I don't write about O. W.—whom I admire immensely—is because the theme is threadbare. I began writing of him in 1889, about the same time that I "discovered" (for myself, at any rate) Shaw and Nietzsche; Ibsen

I had made a study as far back as 1879. Of Wilde I wrote columns for years in the old *Musical Courier*. Oscar saw them for the reason that the London *Musical Courier*, a filiale, reproduced my Raconteur columns. I had met him in Phila. in 1880 or 1881— I forget the date—but I really did not hear him talk, and such marvellous talk, until 1890 or 1891. He was beginning to fall off; rotten print; a peach too long in the sunshine; nevertheless he was simply huge. Better 1,000 times than his books or plays. He said some pleasant things to me, I remember, also several cutting. He looked like a vile Adonis, a beast with swollen lips and heavy jaw, the eyes dull until the man was aroused and then they became phosphorescent. It was a clear case of booze; he drank early and often, champagne, brandy, absinthe. Huysmans he adored.

Yes, I read the poems in *Bang* and liked them; also the rhythmic Wilde and Heine. The latter recalled the metre of Vance Thompson's "I Walked Down Broadway with the Ghost of Poe," first printed in *Mlle. New York;* but of course you never saw it. I liked very much the Sappho; it is full of music and atmosphere—Swinburnean, perhaps. The David is stronger. I hope to see all the fugitive verse in a volume some day. Don't get too many of the old themes between covers. Aren't you going to write for Swinburne an "Ave atque Vale." The *Mirror* I haven't seen for years. Reedy doesn't send it to me.

Excuse long letter. I wish to pay off a few old obligations in the way of acknowledging poems and letters.

Georg Brandes wrote me last week. Did you see my review of Symons's book in *Sun* yesterday (3rd section)?

As ever, sincerely,
JAMES HUNEKER.

George Sylvester Viereck.

To Mrs. Rollins H. Wilbur

The Carrollton
Madison Ave. & 76 St.
June 14, 1909

MY DEAR MADAME:

Thank you for your kind words, the bookplate is charming. The list you sent might, I think, be improved by additions—so as to secure contrasts. After "Madame Bovary" read "Salammbo," after the "Temptation of Saint Anthony" (the early published version—not the newer) read "L'Education Sentimentale," thus gray and gold, purple and sawdust will be well mixed. Flaubert, despite his clear style, contains worlds of irony, disillusionments and philosophies, get both volumes (2) of Gourmont's "Livre des Masques." In the *Sun* this morning I had a little study on the editorial page, "Ideas and Images," of his last book. "Les Illumateais" of Rimbaud is an impossible book; I shan't recommend it—it is unintelligible, otherwise not objectionable, Mallarmé is caviare—French a 1,000 times more difficult than Browning (in English). His verse and prose is in one slender volume. "Vers et Prose" is the title. Rather read Jules La Forge; his "Moralités Legendaire" enchanting in its grace and irony. Of Huysmans' "A Rebours," of Barré's "Le Jardin de Berenice," Turgenieff and all! get either the French edition (better than the English) or the Garnett translation (Macmillan) Dostoievski: "Crime and Punishment"; gruesome, but psychologically sound. "The Idiot," &c. Poieteoin—one book is like another, "Seule" or any one: they are out of print, I hear. Pushkin is in verse. It is translated—reads like a Russian Byron and a trifle faded. Also, as an antiseptic, I find "The Imitation of Christ" by Thomas à Kempis or the "Pilgrim's Progress," by Bunyan. I read a little in one or the other of them every day. They purify. They soothe. Have you read John Galsworthy? "The Man of Property" and "The Country House" or "The Island Pharisee" are worth while. A flavor, an agreeable one of Thackeray exhales from these ironic, sincere pages. I hope this list will fill out your summer. I am at work on my Liszt study—to appear Oct., 1911, the 100th anniversary of the great Hungarian's birthday.

Sincerely, as ever,

Mrs. Rollins H. Wilbur.   JAMES HUNEKER.

To George Sylvester Viereck

The Carrollton
981 Madison Ave.
June 29, 1909

DEAR VIERECK:

I go down town about 2 times a year to the office.
I know no more about the editorial machinery than
you.   In reality I am only a contributor, so you see
I can't answer your very natural question.   I'm sorry.
Who wouldn't be pleased at the spread you gave
me; above all at the title?   Still I must protest.   A
critic—especially an American—is of no particular
importance in the scheme of things.   And thus far
beyond writing words I've done nothing.   The older
I grow the more futile all manner of ink seems.
When one has the lyric gift as you have in a splendid
degree, then you can sing.   I've just had a letter from
Mrs. Symons.   Arthur goes to concerts, theatres, etc.,
but is not much better.   He must be improving to be
able to go out.   No one, I am assured, would notice
anything amiss with him, except his pallor and debil-
ity.   But all this is confidential.

As ever, with renewed thanks,

J. H.

George Sylvester Viereck.

To E. P. Mitchell

The Carrollton
981 Madison Ave.
July 6, 1909

DEAR MR. MITCHELL:

You mustn't think because I do not call or write you that I am none the less sensible of the many favors you do me.   You are a busy man always and I like to think that I am not robbing you of the precious moments—that is not more than I can help.   I sent last Tuesday the book on porcelain (Dr. Burbee's) to you by one of the young men in the lower office.   If you did not receive it will you please notify me. Otherwise I will take it for granted you received the book.   I write now to ask you that, if there is no chance of that story—"The Fabulous East Side"— being used in the *Sun*, if you won't send it up by mail. Apart from its availability as a topic, I fear it is too long—over 2 col. (though it might be split in two if you like the story).   I hardly think I will offer it elsewhere, but I do want, if not the manuscript (there is no hurry for it; it may rest on the hooks six months more) a pull of the galleys.   If you will be so kind. I gave you the story about six months ago, but had not much hope.   Pardon me giving you this bother.   I intend using it in a Spring (1910) book, of lighter calibre than "Egoists", something out of doors sort. Hoping you are well, my dear Mr. Mitchell,

I remain yours, as ever,

JAMES HUNEKER.

Edward P. Mitchell.

To Charles J. Rosebault

Hotel De L'Europe
Brussels, Oct. 11, 1909

DEAR CHARLES:

We were both glad to get your letter yesterday here on our return from Bruges (which is worth all Belgium for beauty—and then the Flemish Primitives, Memling, Van Eyck!) Mr. L. thought I ought to take a rest and I've had one with a vengeance. Three days last week I wrote 21,000 (actually 21,000 words) words for the *Sun* about Holland & the people & pictures. And now today I'm again chained to my room for 2 days where I expect to turn out 12,000 words on Bruges, Antwerp, Ghent, Brussels & Ostende. No fun, no leisure, landed Sept. 11; a perfect drive ever since. Charlie, don't miss Holland and Belgium—particularly Bruges & Antwerp. Brussels is 2nd rate, yet interesting. Mr. M. & Mr. L. were lovely to me, and liberal, but I'm working just 10 times harder than in N. Y. and both the Missus and myself are worn out. We expect to be in Paris by

Friday or perhaps Thursday; but only to take the Paris-Madrid Express, due in Spain not later than Monday 11th inst. That gives us 2 weeks, for we expect to sail Oct. 18 Gibraltar, S.S. Berlin. Farewell to my scheme for England or the pleasure of seeing Bright Eyes, L. D. R. or you. Too bad! But you will be over, I hope, this winter. You may note by this writing the shaky condition of my nerves. Heaven help the *Sun* compositors. Fitz Laffan is, or rather was, in London. Mr. Mitchell is in the south of France. No news otherwise. I'll get mail at Brown, Shipley & Co., 123 Pall Mall, for the next 10 days. Au revoir, with regards from both.

As ever,

JIM.

I feel like a primitive.

Charles J. Rosebault.

To E. E. Ziegler

Dec. 11, 1909, 2.45 A.M.

DEAR NED:

I'm enjoying one of my sleepless nights (I say "enjoy" literally, for I like to go to bed at 8 p. m. and wake at 2 a. m. refreshed with beauty sleep, but not beautiful and, above all, with a lovely thirst!) and hasten to answer your note of yesterday. There is nothing to thank me for, even if you pull the job off.

I couldn't do it and not wishing to play dog in the manger, I suggested you. C. won't, simply won't hear of the elder Triumvirate, K. F. H. &c. Besides that I think it will prove profitable to you to make connections at the magazine. Aber nicht zu bescheiden! ask $200 an article. You may be offered $100. Then split for $150—triumphantly. A joyous dance. However, $200 is better than $150.

Now—Balzac. There is an edition in French, very popular, 50 volumes long, at the very moderate rate of 1 franc a volume: *i. e.* 50 francs for 50 volumes. Nicht theur, was? It may cost more here. Try Brentano or that smiling Dyrssens, 33rd, west of 5th Ave., opposite Waldorf-Astoria. At Brentano's tell your friend to ask for Mr. Ernest Eisele, who will post him, anyhow. Sunst geht gut? I've been up against bad luck. Regards to Suzanne and tell girlie I'm waiting for her to grow up; and then——
(oh my darling!)
à vous! à vous!

Yours nigh to nightmares. As ever,

JIM.

P. S. I'm in Bruges, next Sunday, Madrid. The mills of the printers grind slowly. What?

E. E. Ziegler.

To Mrs. Charles H. Ditson

Sunday, Dec. 14

MY DEAR MRS. DITSON:

I am sorry you think that I got up a little attack to avoid keeping my engagement. The fact is I have had a hellish cold—something new for me—since Thursday night. I'm better now and sorry I could not see you yesterday. I return the matter you sent me. The copy I corrected is, of course, the better one. But it is very verbose, and that clause about subscribers voting for a conductor—what idiocy! Do you want Frank Damrosch or Wetzler, or F. X. Arens, or the most popular of all—Franz Kaltenborn? That's what a ballot system would do. Better engage a big man in Europe and then say: "Here, damn you! here he is; you've got to take him." Then ram him down their stupid throats. I'll drop in this week.

As ever,

JAMES HUNEKER.

Mrs. Charles H. Ditson.

To George Sylvester Viereck

The Carrollton
981 Madison Ave.
April 25, 1910

DEAR VIERECK:

Here are a few words which if you care to you may use for your book. (The fewer the better say I, in cases of this sort.) Please *don't* credit them to the *Sun,* or mention that journal, as I am not a book reviewer. I fancy it would be more advisable to simply let the enclosed be "ungültig"—just as if I sent you a wireless. And please don't cut out too much. The book pleased me. I finished it in German. I finished it Saturday evening at one sitting. The chapter on "Gambrinuss" made me thirst. I thought of "Ewige Lampe," where I have never been. Some mad June night I'll make my will, arm myself heavily and start for that delectably named place. It must be in the jungle of the Bronx or Harlem. But I'll go. *Gratulire!*

As ever,

JAMES HUNEKER.

P. S. Is there such a place, or is it only a myth of the Vorkaempen?

(Note enclosed)

GEORGE SYLVESTER VIERECK

The spectacle of young Viereck spanking two nations in his "Confessions of a Barbarian" is enough to arouse the marble bust of his once famous grandmother, Edwina Viereck, at the Royal Theater, Berlin; to stir the envy of the first and only Shavian, G. B. S. George Sylvester Viereck is the head of a long line of American Super-Boys. . . His book is flown with the frank insolence and effervescing wine of brilliant youth. . . He knows, like most poets, absolutely nothing of men and women, of art or life, and that is his chief charm. The fires of inexperience are more creative than the slag and cinders of wisdom. . . Truth has been known to pop forth from the mouths of babes.

JAMES HUNEKER.

To George Sylvester Viereck

The Carrollton
981 Madison Ave.
April 29, 1910

DEAR VIERECK:

The few lines were written with an eye on the "general reader." Privately I believe nothing of the kind. Your book is uncanny in its wealth of general wisdom. You must be at least 119 years old, and

MRS. JAMES HUNEKER

didn't you come into the world with whiskers? As I wrote yesterday to a well-known literary editor who is, by reason of his temperament, bound to state the book: "With all his pose of egoism, etc., etc. G. S. V. contrives to say just the things for which an author writing solemnly would be denounced as an enemy of society. American *henchlerei*, rum, women, disgusting voting animals, etc., are all dealt with the touch of a fencing master—one whose blade has been dipped in venom," etc. (all this, of course, confidential). Ewige Lampe, some Saturday afternoon, Was? Grüsse,   As ever,

                                        J. H.

George Sylvester Viereck.

To E. E. Ziegler

Sunday, May 20, 1910

DEAR EDWARD:

Why so violent! No bones are broken, and we can all meet some time later. What has Blumenberg to do with the case, anyhow? Apart from the fact that I only spoke to him, standing, not even drinking with him for 5 minutes, there is no sinister significance in our accidental recounter. He did not speak of you! Why drag him in? And the reason I did not see you was, to be plain, Ned, it behoved your Uncle James to stir his old pins and hustle for cash. So I saw *no one*, went nowhere. I've been out twice

since I saw you: once, the mild whirl with Shelley
and Gregg; twice with Mrs. Huneker at Lüchow's.
Last Saturday week when we met Otto for 20 minutes. I had left the doctor's where my ancient hulk
was sentenced and I begged for just one more pilsner. I got it. I paid up for it for my gout went to
the eyes. Behold my miscroscopic writing! I was
glad to see Shelley after so many years. I like him,
you don't. I like Otto. He is not a bad fellow, and
as to music, there are few who can tie his shoe strings
in this town. (Don't grind your teeth, Bill!) He
told me he spent a pleasant afternoon with Krehbiel.
The old matter is not by any means adjusted.
Bloomy, when I saw him at Schulz's on B'way—I
don't know where Churchill's is; never been there—
told me he had O. F. "fixed." He also told me I was
still a stockholder, and when I said "put up the cash,"
he went away. That's all! Nor were we at Jack's,
but with Gregg and Harry at the Manhattan Hotel
café! It was all very quiet. What a crowd of
"mollies," waschweib,—Chin-choppers, tittle-tattles
you meet, Edward! There was no secrecy. Shelley
could tell all that happened. What a little town—
especially the musical end of it! I suppose I'm free
to see any one I desire. Floersheim told me the *M. C.*
had a roast of "Visionaries." I didn't see it, and I
am too indifferent to get a copy. So much for Blumenberg stories. Which I hope you will contradict.
The table *is* too small for 4 and I don't like you to

contradict me on the subject. If it were not, we should have asked you both to dinner long ago. And you could have easily picked out a night; you are not going to stand on ceremony at this late day. However, let's drop the rot—I go to Phila. the 25th. When I return I'll drop you a line about a luncheon engagement. I haven't seen Marsh for months. Am I busy? You'll see me, boy. Regards from house to house—lucky dog to own one.

As ever,

JIM.

E. E. Ziegler.

To Mrs. Rollins H. Wilbur

The Carrollton
981 Madison Ave.
June 29, 1910

MY DEAR MRS. WILBUR:

I enclose card with my autograph in case you do not care to send over the book. The card can be pasted in it. However, if that will not serve by all means send the book. I'll return it at once. No, I've not been in Europe since Dec. last, nor do I see any prospect of being away anywhere until my Franz Liszt is finished; it is supposed to be on the market by Oct., 1911, the anniversary date of Liszt's birth. But I have my doubts. The task is a trying one, for I must turn out my daily stuff for the *Sun*, so as to eat my bread. Someone has said that surplus—or overflow—is genius; then I'm none, as I need all of mine merely to eke out a living. You say you saw no articles of mine in the *Sun*. Well, here are two that appeared last Sunday. I write on various topics during the summer; seldom on music. Usually review books.

You are very kind to take the interest you do in my little books. I secured the Bruges post cards with pleasure.

Sincerely yours,
Jim Huneker.

Mrs. Rollins H. Wilbur.

To E. P. Mitchell

The Carrollton
981 Madison Ave.
Dec. 8, 1910

Dear Mr. Mitchell:

I saw the new Veronese yesterday and was, if not completely conquered, still very much impressed. As the story of its acquisition has already appeared in the news columns I think I'll wait a few days before writing a special notice, wait in fact, until the appearance of the December *Bulletin*, which will contain the news of the other acquisitions—a remarkable Canaletto, which has not yet been put on view. The beginning of next week we are promised these things and then I'll make my regular monthly Metr. Museum story.

The L. catalogue after 10 days' wrestling with the devils of attribution is finished—all except the brief introduction, which I hope to submit to you as soon as I can after my return from Washington. I have decided to go next Thursday, Dec. 15. I will stop on my return at Phila., and see the Winslow Homers at the Water Color show (Penn. Academy), and the Art Club exhibition of American Artists over which John McFadden is the presiding spirit. I, perchance, Sunday, Dec. 18th, could see the J. G. Johnson collection—then I could bring down four birds with one trip! But that particular affair doesn't much matter, as I could be always ready to go over when Mr. J. would see fit—supposing, of course, that he will be so amiable.

Sincerely yours,
JAMES HUNEKER.

E. P. Mitchell.

P. S.—The "Academy"—that assemblage of stupid or mediocre pictures—opens on Saturday next. I'll send down a story early Monday.

To John Quinn

The Carrollton
Aug. 10, 1911

DEAR QUINN:

I write in haste so as to catch you before you leave
on the B. B. route for Portland. 1st; Thanks for the
Greco, which I'll hardly have time to tackle before I
leave. 2nd; also for the letter of Shannon which
rings sincere; though he doesn't wield the pen of
Gus John. As to your very kind invitation for Long
Beach I fear it can't be pulled off. Apart from the
fact that I can't spare the night, I'm in a bad way
with toothache, swollen face and eye strain—the
latter has affected my stomach and nerves. Too
much reading and writing, and the horrible heats of
July. I've not tasted beer since June 23rd, the night
we were out. For once my good old tank has re-
volted. And horrible to relate, I'm still reading proof
on the *Liszt!* This job of only 125,000 words was
delayed by the printers. It has upset all my plans
for sailing on Aug. 19th. I'm lucky if I get off Aug.
26th. We propose to go to Antwerp—Bruges, rest
there; then to Cologne, and follow a regular round
of German art galleries as far south as Munich, perhaps Prague & Vienna—certainly the latter two, if
I attend the Liszt Festival at Budapest Oct. 22nd. A
big order all this—as yet a pipe dream. But we
hope! Therefore, all things considered, my dear

Quinn, you will have to let us out this time, and we both sorrow! Hope you have a good time. Dodge Paris. It's rotten, noisy, dusty, hot. My book will be out in Oct. The article on Liszt is to appear in October number *Scribner's* magazine. In 10 days the burden—indeed an old man of the C—will be off my shoulders. Then I'll breathe—if the dentist leaves me a mouth to breathe with. He has just pulled 2 molars, and another is to follow. Hell hath no, &c. Mrs. Huneker sends regards. So do I.

As ever,

JAMES HUNEKER.

John Quinn.

To Henry T. Finck

The Carrollton
981 Madison Ave.
Nov. 5, 1911

DEAR HARRY:

Excuse the delay in acknowledging your letter which I've just read. We are back from Germany only one day, I with two broken ribs, the souvenir of a fall in Cologne Sep. 20;—a zealous railway *Träger* having placed some hand luggage at the steps of our carriage. So my vacation is curtailed. I missed Budapest as well as Heidelberg, though I

went to Berlin often. Three weeks on my back in
Cassel. I'm still sick. Your notice of the Liszt (a
botched book, by the way) was bully. I thank you.
I'm not a *Lisztianer.* I loathe his piano music—
with a few exceptions. The Poems and Dante, Faust
and the Masses are the real Liszt. However, I let
others do him justice. I've his complete works in
French and German. I've not read them once but
20 times (the *Courier* file will prove this); I detest
him as a writer as much as I love him as a man. In
a word, Harry, I got *"cold feet";* my book should
have appeared in 1902 when my enthusiasm hadn't
cooled. All criticism is so futile to me that I've not
done the theme justice. Saw the Spanuths in Berlin.
August sends greetings. He is an important man there
and is busy, very. When I've seen a surgeon I'll
run up and see you—you surgeon of criticism! But
I'm so glad to get even a line from you. I'm miserable in body and spirit. A splendid tour inter-
rupted by fate. (I would laugh but I can't.)

Regards to Mrs. Finck.

As ever

JIM.

How did you like the head of F. L. in the frontis-
piece?

Henry T. Finck.

To E. P. Mitchell

The Carrollton
981 Madison Ave.
Nov. 23, 1911

DEAR MR. MITCHELL:

I should be presenting this enclosed copy to you in person, but I still balk at stair climbing—my breathing not yet being normal—and I'm sure you will excuse me until next week when I shall climb or perish in the attempt. I'm better—for I've had a rest I never contemplated, this being the first time I've written since I was in Bruges. The editorial speaks for itself; the George Moore story—which is hardly a book review—is apropos just now, because the Irish Players and Lady Gregory are in town; also because the book is not on this side of the Atlantic, and has not been widely reviewed in Great Britain. At all events I submit the story, as the anecdotes and portraiture in "Ave" are wonderfully acute and comical. I hope you are well, and I further hope you got away this Fall.

Sincerely yours,

JAMES HUNEKER.

Edward P. Mitchell.

To Mrs. Samuel W. Moore

The Carrollton
981 Madison Ave.
Sunday, Dec. 10, 1911

DEAR AUNT AUBERTINE:

I'm sorry I didn't preserve my bound volumes of
the *Musical Courier*. I'm glad, as a rule, to forget
what I wrote during the practice years. But I still
vividly remember the W. W. episodes. I met Walt
in 1877, Camden, Mickle St. Just before I ran away
to Paris (if I recollect aright, ran off to see Liszt!).
When I returned in 1880 I saw W. W. occasionally.
The Spring of 1880 or 1881, Carl Gaertner gave his
series in the foyer of the Academy of Music, South
Broad St. He did play the sextette op. 20 of Beethoven, and I remember the, to me, always thrilling variation with the horn, in the variation movement—the
minor one, I mean. Walt was there, and I walked to
the Market St. cars with him, and saw him safely
east bound for the ferry. "So long, young fellow,"
he called out to me from the platform. I saw him
later, but that night I remember with alarming dis-
tinctness, when I wrote his obituary for the now de-
funct N. Y. *Home Journal*, I forgot to mention the
occurrence. It is of slight value yet may stir your
recollections. I'm doing a series of German cities
for the Sunday *Sun*, editorial page. Last Sunday

Cologne & Cassell; today, Frankfort & Darmstadt; next week—perhaps—Berlin. Only art.

With best wishes for the season, I am your old friend,

JAMES HUNEKER.

Mrs. Samuel Woodward Moore.

To E. E. Ziegler

The Carrollton
981 Madison Ave.
Dec. 18, 1911

DEAR NED:

(Don't start so suddenly!)

Do you think it would be possible (steady) for you to get me (2) oh god!! seats for the Philharmonic Society next Friday afternoon, the Liszt-Dante affair I mean. I read about the work in a new book about Liszt published by the Scribners. It looks good to me—the programme I mean: and then, Arthur Friedheim in the A. major. If you can't (don't shy at that!) let me know and I'll pay, be god! I want to show a little attention to my Missus—who nursed me so loyally in Cologne (near the Ewige Lampe, where they fill the wicks with pilsner). She is quite a patient girl. I saw the counterfet presentment of Suzanne Ziegler and missy on 5th Ave. a week or so ago, Caruso almost treading on her head. That's a pretty good photograph. If it, and yours ever found

their way up here, they would be warmly welcomed
for the collection—especially if autographed. (This
isn't a hint, is it), seriously, Edward, if the tickets
are not forthcoming to you let me hear, and I'll try
elsewhere, which doesn't sound polite, but you know
what I mean (I never have to explain to you), what's
the bad or good word. I just dote on work. But I
must hear that programme, and also Stransky. The
Spanuths are very nicely settled in Berlin. I loathe
the town, prefer Frankfort or Munich, but I fancy I'll
end my days in dear, dirty old New York. Sorry
you didn't turn up Saturday a week ago. When shall
we three meet again, Macbeth.

As ever,

JIM.

Edward E. Ziegler.

To Mrs. Rollins H. Wilbur

The Carrollton
981 Madison Ave.
Dec. 28, 1911

MY DEAR MRS. WILBUR:
    With the charming instrument* of torture you so
kindly sent me (for I loathe pen and ink as much as
I loathe all forms of hard labor), I'm thanking you,
and wishing a Happy New Year. Also I again re-

* Pen holder made of a crow feather from Stratford
Churchyard.

gret my inability to travel. (In this same mail I'm writing to Mr. Burmeister how sorry I was to have missed hearing his "favorite pupil," Conradi.)

Sincerely, as ever,

JAMES HUNEKER.

To Charles J. Rosebault

The Carrollton
981 Madison Ave.
April 24, 1912

DEAR CHARLES:

I'm just beginning to breathe. The season is over, and now how about a meeting of the Quartette internationale? Mrs. Huneker is in the hands of the dentist Thursday. I go to the same executioner Friday afternoon.

Would Saturday night be too short notice for Mrs. Rosebault and you? If so let us make it next week, any time after Wed. night; preferably Sat., 11th, inst. Just ourselves this trip. I don't want to miss you before you sail. When do you leave? Or will you stay over this summer. We go in August, and to England, instead of the usual continental trip. I've news for you, and I want to bother you with questions, lots of them. So let us hear any time within the next 3 days. Bring your thirst along. Regards to Mrs. Rosebault from Mrs. Huneker—not forgetting myself.

As ever,

JIM.

Charles J. Rosebault.

To Grenville Vernon

Westminster Court
1618 Beverly Road, Brooklyn
April 19/12

MY DEAR VERNON:

I'm obliged to you for your kindness. But for
heaven's sake don't hurry Mr. James. I had sus-
pected that he was rushed; only, I feared my letters
had gone astray. Of course, I'll be glad to get those
precious letters again. As to H. E. K. I hope he will
not get in the dumps again; but my lad, it's hard to
be shunted off the rails after 40 years' work. And
in my early days he was the Czar of music—criticism,
though a benignant Czar. His mind has been benefi-
cent, and need I add, luminous! We must, all of
us, step aside. Every critic has his hour. And he is
specially blessed. As I wrote him, I wish some newspaper would insist on putting me out "to pension."
What joy! Now I'm usually dropped after the juice
has been squeezed from the orange. A warning—a
long way ahead—to you G. V. Esq. Sensible chaps
usually get under cover by 40; or on the band-wagon.
I'm in Flatbush surrounded by cemeteries, baby car-
riages, funerals every 10 minutes, and the Rachmani-
noff C sharp minor Prelude played by Flatbush flap-
pers on every floor of this apartment—which has not
the marmoreal calm of the Abbey in London. The
Tribune I find good reading. The editorials are ex-

cellent, and R. Cortissoz is simply spiffling on Sundays. All the departments are brilliant. I read the paper daily instead of its neighbor. So why complain, especially if you get your pay envelope. I'm eating the air—"promise crammed"—and playing Bach.

Selah! With thanks.

As ever,

JAMES HUNEKER.

Grenville Vernon.

To Theodore Presser

N. Y., June 3, 1912

DEAR PRESSER:

I'm sorry I missed you last Monday, but it was unavoidable, and on me the blame rests. We—Mrs. Huneker with me—went to 1712 when you were at luncheon; we couldn't get there sooner because we took a later train from Browns Mills in the Pines, N. J. (where my brother has a bungalow) Monday; left sooner than we had expected. Hence the delay. The heat knocked out the Missus, and we went over to New York on the earliest train we could catch. But I hope to get over before I leave in August. However, here is the situation. I'll be satisfied with the price ($50) you mention for the O. F.* articles.

* "Old Fogy."

Please let me know about the number of words. I note in the June *Etude* the announcement of an August kick-over-the-milk-pail-and-raise-hell, joyful number. About when should I send in a story (O. F. of course)? Next item: You say that it will not take many more papers (O. F.) to make up a book. Have you the complete set? I have 18, no more. I didn't count the number of words, but I presume a small book that would retail at $1 or $1.25 would be better than a bulkier volume. You know, Theodore, that sort of fun soon palls, especially between covers. And what percentage will you allow me on the net price? I now get from Scribner's (this is confidential, but I can show my last contract) 15 percent. On the Liszt, a $2 volume, that netted me 30 cents a copy. Not bad! Furthermore, would you be willing after all proofs are read and returned, to advance me on the expected royalties, $500, cold American cash? I have another idea to submit to you. If an Old Fogy book is brought out, the old chap must be definitely killed. You can't keep that venerable Manayunk Mummy forever gasbagging about Bach. In that case whether the cat escapes from the bag or not doesn't much matter. Now here is my scheme—subject to your editorial and business judgment. Why not get up a title page something like this:

Musical Memories of the Late

OLD FOGY

(1723-1913)

Being a collection of his wit and wisdom, prejudices and theories of the Johann Sebastian Buxehude of Manayunk and Weimar.

Revised and edited, with an introduction (or 'short biography) by his old friend and former pupil,

JAMES HUNEKER

—Something of the sort—we shall have to give the old codger a local habitation and a name, and the fact that my name will be on the title page, won't hurt the sale of the book. But if you wish to keep up the anonymity game, all right. The above is only my notion. Of course, I'll devise a more attractive title page; also a fine mediocre head for a portrait must be found. I'll get one—a fancy head; naturally. Take your leisure in answering this, and cover all the points I raise. Later we can discuss the matter over 2½ pilsners in Phila. (the ½ is for you; the 2 for me, as I am the thirstier brother).

As ever,

JIM HUNEKER.

Theodore Presser.

To Theodore Presser

N. Y., July 13, 1912

DEAR THEODORE:

Thank you for the Old Fogy Cheque. I'll let you know two or three days ahead of my next visit to Phila. I'm glad if we can get the book "over," as they say in theatrical circles. I'll read the contract carefully; it is presumably the same form as the Scribner contracts—of which since 1899 I've signed just 10. I'll bring over the Old Fogy matter with me, and edited; also the extra matter of which I spoke, this latter subject to your judgment. Perhaps the volume won't need any padding at all. I'll also bring the introduction—signed, and the projected title-page. The amount of royalty we can fix up at our ease. I'm not difficult, as you may realize when I tell you that until my 9th book (The "Franz Liszt") I never got more than 10 per cent on the published price. Now I get 15 per cent. *Höchste Zeit!* as Schopenhauer wrote when he read Wagner's stage directions for a "quick curtain" fall at the close of the 1st act of "Die Walküre"! But I should very much like—and this is a more important matter—to get an advance royalty. In the case of such a small book as "Old Fogy" a small sum will suffice, say $500. Its always more satisfactory to the "poor author" to get a nibble in advance. But, again, we will settle this viva voce. Don't bother sending page proof of August "Old Fogy" unless there are queries.

The galley proof read clean, and I made few cor-
rections. I hope you are keeping cool. I am not
though I'm writing in my pyjamas on a 10th floor.
To hell with the heat; that's where it belongs. Adieu!
With regards,
JAMES HUNEKER.
Theodore Presser.

To Theodore Presser

The Carrollton
New York City
July 31st, 1912

DEAR PRESSER:

It wouldn't do any good to write to C. S. & S. for
the simple reason that even if they should consent
(and they wouldn't), I would not. You want something for nothing, and I wouldn't let my name go for
$250. It's worth more to me. However, that's neither
here nor there, the cases are not in the least alike, and
I don't mind telling you that it would not be exactly
a good move to say outright—as you wish to—that
I am the author of Old Fogy. Don't you see, that
apart from the fact that all the fun of the thing—or
joke—would evaporate if I put my name to the book
—that also the little mystery of Old Fogy's personality would quite vanish! To sign my name to so
many senile and puerile opinions would seem strange.
But with a provoking preface, the joke would be a
vital, not a flat one. I can easily weave a fictitious

biography and everyone who reads will understand that I'm having fun with my old opinions, just letting off gas for the sake of being contradictory. No, my name must not be signed. Now, as you find it difficult to meet me half-way, let me make a final suggestion—and then close the matter. I hope to sail Sat., Aug. 17; and am so rushed that I can't get over to Phila., where I'm sure we could have settled this tremendously "important" matter in 15 minutes. Here's my scheme, and last offer: I have two plans in my head for 2 more Old Fogys—one is serious (that is serious in his more sincere manner); the other is a rather comical idea—a college for music-critics, with the account of an examination—the papers, etc., all the names thinly disguised (our best known) music critics of course, no offence given, no disagreeable personalities, just fun. These 2 stories I'll dictate as I fear my handwriting for proof, especially, as I won't be in America next winter. You can use them in the *Etude* before the book appears. Furthermore, I'll furnish an Introduction, and send you with it the 17 copies of Old Fogy, I've saved, edited, and arranged in order. Also two (2) possible reprints from publications (one out of print, the other printed in 1890, therefore exempt from copyright restrictions; both merely submitted to your judgment for the book alone), and all this I'll give you for $250 with the understanding of course that my name is not to go as author. By this arrangement you will get $100 worth of "copy"—2 stories for Old Fogy, in *Etude*—and this leaves only $150 to me literally in advance. How's that? Come now, Theodore, be a sport even if you do hail from old penurious Phila. Nothing risked, nothing won, and if you can't risk $150 net on me, why then let's drop the transaction for good. I'll make up a simple effective title page for you (there need be no table of contents), and if you let me have an answer to this by Saturday morning, Aug. 3rd, I'll send you over by Tuesday, next, the entire shooting match. But that cheque must be for $250 (you will be getting $100 of this in the goods delivered).

As ever,

JIM.

Theodore Presser.

To John Quinn

The Carrollton
August 1st, 1912

DEAR JOHN:

I found your letter here, a few hours after I wired you. I do hope you didn't mistake my message as indecent haste. We both believed you were to sail next Sat., and I saw the event slipping—hence my urgency. Now, as you are to be here next week, even—perhaps—Saturday, the 10th inst., we can make the date more at leisure. You know you are a "rusher," and more than apt to pack your trunk over night and sail of a morning than to go off at moderate notice. However, the main thing is settled; the pictures are at your house, the four boxes—which appalled me by their size; I only take 500 books along, and I really believe I can get them in one box— so many are paper (French and German). I note what you say about the "holes"; also that "menstruel" allusion—almost as bad as the Madem lyric version of Moore (?) "The Minstrual Boy (Play) to the whore has gone." Didn't you once say, the Kelt to speak rich, evil vocables. A letter from London informs me that Fitz Laffan is there, and daily expecting McCloy; so I fancy Greggo is up to his eyes in work. Of course, after John, Matisse, A. B. Davies, the soft velvety belly and gracious contours of the Besnard drawing seem a trifle conventional; above all, lacking in "tactile values"; nevertheless, there is the charm of adolescence, the sense of the unruptured hymen, which the three men mentioned above never do—or could—suggest. I'm sorry I can't use the Eugenic allusion somewhere; it's good enough for the Pope to smile—let us hope, sacerdotally.

Now here is a proposition, Quinn, my Jo John. Why not sail with us on the "Finland," Aug. 17th— next Saturday, two weeks. You'll never get away on the 10th (Sat. a week); indeed, I'll be quite surprised to see you back by that time from the West. We could have a hell of a fine time—in ten days you land

in Boulogne, all the good beer drunk up on board,
long confabs, good cookery (Belgian), clean berth.
Think it over, John.

As ever,

JIM.

John Quinn.

To E. P. Mitchell

Westminster Court
Brooklyn, Nov. 12/12

MY DEAR MR. MITCHELL:

May I ask for the privilege of proof for enclosed
story—which is as full of modern instances as ancient saws. I shall esteem it a personal favor. My
handwriting, I know, is hopeless, yet the mistakes,
purely typographical I hope, in my printed stuff are
becoming alarming. The Mallock story was dis-
figured by such breaks as "Intention," when I wrote
of Bergson's "Intuition." I am, I know, to blame;
but worse follows: In the "New York of the Novel-
ists" (Sunday, Nov. 5th), from De Quincey's
"Opium Eater" was sadly misquoted. Any school-
girl knows it, "Oxford Street, Stony-hearted Step-
mother." It came out "Strong" in print! Now on the
same page was "Emma Bovary's Tomb" right. It
masked as "Touch"; nor was Henry Harland's "The
Yoke of the Torah" spared. It was printed Torch,
but there is excuse for this as the Hebrew "Torah"

(sacred scroll) is an unusual word for a fiction tale. E titti quanti! However, as I am not expected to turn in copy any particular day, and, if it won't incommode the machinery of the office, I should very much like to have a peep at my proof once in a while. I promise to return it promptly; also not to make any additions; only to correct, if there are any excisions to be made, and I am told my copy is so and as many lines too long, then I could make them with a reasonable confidence. The Mallock story had all the personal quality extracted by the forceps of an accomplished dental surgeon. This wail will, I hope, reach sympathetic ears. What do you think of a correspondent's suggestion (sometime in last week's issue), that a "Gourmet's Guide to N. Y." be written. Couldn't it be done in 2 cols. over my initials?

Sincerely
JAMES HUNEKER.

Edward P. Mitchell.

To Mme. Frida Ashforth

Westminster Court
Brooklyn, N. Y.
Dec. 19/12

YOU DEAR FRIDA:

The picture actually made me homesick. A peaceful, but vanished time! It stands on my desk where I now face it as I enter. Thank you, old pal!

I hope "Unicorns" arrived. I had a lovely letter from Maurice Maeterlinck this morning about the book. I'll save it for your eyes. I arrived home this morning at 3:15 a. m. from Phila. on special Met. Opera House Train. Florence Easton made an enormous hit last night over there as—Santuzza. A singing actress. Temperament! But is smashing her voice by forcing—already upper tones pinched, colorless. A big voice at that. But an actress—like Calvé! Fancy! An English woman—wife of the American Tenor Francis McLennan, who formerly sang Wagner roles in Berlin and Hamburg. Caruso as *Canio!* is there ever an end to that glorious organ. He is a bellows on legs, and a jolly, kind chap.

However, I'm tired out today. I had to write a column before our train left—and a column about such stuff—musically speaking—as Mascagni and Leon—on the—Cavallo Basta!

With love from both and again thanks for a unique Christmas present.

Merry Christmas!

Yours, as ever,

JIM, the HUNEKER.

(or, as they now say, "Hunekerkorus")

Frida Ashforth.

Photograph by Sargent

JAMES HUNEKER

Taken about 1895

To Charles J. Rosebault

DeKeyser's Royal Hotel,
London E.C., England
8.30 p.m., 1913

DEAR CHARLES:

Only a line to say we came back from Harrowgate (after a week to recuperate from the terrific heat here the week before) last night, and today I found your post card and letter. You will understand my delay today in answering yours when I tell you we leave at 8:30 tomorrow (Thursday), for Dublin via Holyhead, for several weeks. (I have 3 stories ordered.) I received your country letters on arrival from Ostend—just at the beginning of the heat; such a change. To tell the truth London is less and less to my taste— I dislike it, and adore its magnificence, but I suppose my nerves are on edge—we are both worn to the bone with fatigue—travel and trunks—and the Missus says if we don't soon head for home, I can head for Hell—alone. New York is so alluring in July and August. We are very sorry to miss you this month, but hope to have better luck next. Send your address to 123 Pall Mall (where I found your letter this morning, and thank you for your bother), and at least I can write you. I sent "Pathos of Distance" to Raymond, Pynchon & Co., before I got your letter. It came out late. New York notices are corkers, but it can't sell very well; it is a $2 book.

It appears here I note in the London papers soon
(Werner Laurie); I hope you like it. It's very personal especially the chapter "How Widor played in
Saint Sulpice." I asked the London agent of the
Etude to send Mrs. Bright Eyes a copy of a book I
edited, and for which I wrote a preface. It is old
time musical views. It may amuse her (or you!)

Regards to both of you from Mrs. Huneker, and

As ever,

JIM.

Charles J. Rosebault.

To Charles J. Rosebault

Park Hotel,
Charlottenburg, Germany
March 12, 1913

DEAR CARL:

Your welcome letter arrived this A. M. and I
hasten to answer it. Thanks for the clippings, the
very two I wished to see, as I can now strike a critical balance 'twixt Finck and Aldrich, and from my
own opinion. Rostand, as you may have heard, is
furious at Henderson and Damrosch, and the Berlin
papers as well as the Paris abuse them as if they
were a pair of pickpockets. Glad to hear you are
contemplating a trip to Spain—try to get to Seville
first, though you will be too late for the interesting
Easter series, as the festival falls so early this year.

But Seville and Cordova (not to mention the Alhambra) and Toledo are worth while. Don't miss *Toledo* —it's the most original city in Europe with the sole exception of Prague. Madrid is mediocre—save the Prado gallery. Go to Hotel Ingles in Madrid— otherwise at the Ritz or Palace you will have to pay by the nose. For 50 francs a day *for both,* you get board as well as a big room. Eating out is not indulged in in Madrid, as the hotel cooking is the better; besides Cafes are not nice, not always clean, and few waiters speak English. We found the Ingles excellent; W. W. Chase, the painter, always goes there. 50 pesetas (francs) is not too much, wine inclusive. If Signor Gomez is manager, as he was in 1909, mention Chase's name; mine he has probably forgotten. Go to Paris via Hendaya on the *luxe* train—26 hours from Madrid to Paris. It's the only way, and it's damnably dear; other trains are crawlers, dirty, smoky, station food rotten. If you tell me you have been in Spain and missed Toledo, I'll cut you dead. The Alhambra is all very well, but it's gimcrack operatic compared with the rugged Toledo.

Now, Charles, on receipt of this, drop me a line, on a postal if you choose, to tell me where I shall send you my new book, due to be published about the middle or end of April. It's called "The Pathos of Distance" (*i.e.,* distance lends enchantment to the view), and is of course, a phrase of Nietzsche. The book is very personal. And various mixed pickles.

I suppose care Raymond, Pynchon & Co., would be the safest address to send to. But let me know.

Don't write here again, only to care Brown Shipley & Co., 123 Pall Mall, W. C., as we may go soon to Brussels; then to Ireland—a comparatively unexploited country from the newspaper point of news. I'm reading galley proofs of my book—4,000 miles away from the printer—hardly a satisfactory thing. Also—my German "Chopin" (to appear May, Georg Müller verlag, Munich & Leipsic), is bothering me. Proofs in German! They call them *bogen.* Wow! But as Müller is one of the liveliest publishers here— I must be careful. The "Chopin" *may sell*—think of that. Keep the matter dark. I won't be certain till the book appears. The *Saturday Review* people wrote me to New York making an offer, but I'll think it over seriously. I'm tired of newspapering. Your news column was very interesting. So Chester Lord has left the *Sun.* It's like "Hamlet" without Hamlet. How does the paper look and read. I suppose Mitchell will be the next. McCloy number 3. It's bound to come, Bill Reick wants cheap people. Do you ever see my *Times* stuff? How is it liked by Dithmar and the office folks? No one to tell me over here, except my press clipping bureau, and to judge by the numerous clippings the articles must be read; they are so frequently quoted. If they printed the Frank Wedekind story I do hope you read it. It cost me sweat. W. is a remarkable man and dramatist. "Frühlings Erwachen" is heart-rending, and the other one-act pieces—bully! He is thrice as original as Sudermann, and witty and devilish. A scandal breeder. We saw and heard and talked with Arthur Nikisch at the last Philharmonic concert. A great man indeed, but his Berlin band is mediocre compared with the glorious Vienna Philharmonic. Opera poor here, much bad piano playing. We shall be glad to leave if only to escape the German cuisine —heavy, flavorless after Austria. Oh for a cup of Vienna coffee. I've written my Prague and Vienna stories (illustrated), but when they will appear, I can't say. In the *Metropolitan* magazine for March. I pay my respects to the Italian Futurists (also illustrated). My Bergson article, another humbug, is due in the March or April *Forum*. Tell Ben we saw the new Herman Bahr play "Das Prinzip" with Else Lehmann as the cook—it's not a second "Concert" as it has only one act—the 2nd—that would go in America; but Lehmann! A woman that stabs your entrails with pity when she plays Rose Bernd (Hauptmann), and is so comical as a Viennese cook who adores waltzing—what versatility. The kitchen scene is a novel setting; otherwise I can't see the piece in English unless violently dislocated.

Pardon the rigmarole, I'm practising 2 hours daily on a fairly bad German "Grand"—nothing but Handel (the E minor fugue) Schumann (the Toccato), and the C major study of Rubinstein. I'm seriously studying tone-production (spiel mit gewichts the war cry nowadays) and trying to shake my Parisian staccato touch. Vergeblich! Regards to Mrs. Rosebault from both. When shall we four meet again—at Paganini's or Odone's? We will be in London from May 1st on.

As ever,

JIM.

Charles J. Rosebault.

To Charles J. Rosebault

Dublin, June 15, 1913

[Postal]

There is here the finest public gallery of modern French Art in Europe, with the exception of the Luxembourg—and they have two better Manet's than at the L. A. charming old-world town.

Greetings from the Happy Homeless Hunekers.

To Mrs. Charles H. Ditson

Amsterdam, Holland
Sept. 7, 1913

DEAR MRS. DITSON:

We knew you were in Europe for we read of you in the *American Detective* abroad, otherwise the Paris (N. Y.) *Herald*. We only wished we could have seen you and Mr. Ditson. The Damrosches too

—we missed, but saw Rudolph Schirmer last May in Brussels—from afar, as he was with a lady, his daughter, I think. July 1st, with the thermometer at 95 degrees, saw us panting on a New York Hudson river deck with a dozen pieces of baggage to be examined. After a few weeks in that Summer hell of steel, stone and horrid sweating humanity we escaped here, where I had to come because of the Peace Palace and Andy Carnegie's attempt to make over the world. I saw the little conjuror with his white head and happy smile sitting on the lap of royalty, Aug. 28th. It was a great dull, humid occasion, and again I dreamt of Ecclesiastes, and the remarks of the mighty Preacher. Did you see in the *Times* last Winter, my account of the music—new indeed, of Arnold Schoenberg? Well, I prefer Schoenberg's music to the tepid glory of the peace palace. The phrase ("tower of ivory") was coined by Sainte-Beuve in one of his *Causeries de Lundi* and in an article on Alfred de Vigny, the disdainful "precious" poet of his day. I utilized it in my "Egoists" for Maurice Barrés—also Pater. I haven't the "Pathos" with me here, but I fancied I had included the Brownings—an ideal union of spirits. When I see you next Winter—and we both are hoping that we may—I'll try to prove that music, emotionally speaking, bone of our bones and flesh of our flesh, is more subjective than even poetry—it is certainly more sexual. My "Chopin" appears Oct. in Munich in German dress;

others follow.   I wax wealthy on royalties.   (We
shall probably be forced to return in the steerage!
With regards from both to you and Mr. Ditson.
I am as ever

>   Yours,
>   JAMES HUNEKER.

Mrs. Charles H. Ditson.

To Charles J. Rosebault

>   Hotel Des Pays Bas
>   Utrecht, Holland
>   Sept. 9, 1913

DEAR CHARLES:

We reached here from Amsterdam yesterday—
which noisy city we fled because of the heat and Mosquitoes (yes, the singing stinging devils were almost
as bad as New York, and that says much for of all
the horrible 6 weeks we ever put in, we passed from
July 1st to Aug. 12 last).   I had to be in The Hague
for Aug. 28 the Peace Palace humbuggery and the
ensuing conference (a lot of grafters!)   Then we
came up to Amsterdam, but spent most of our time
at Zandvoort on the sea and at Haarlem.   Now I
must sit down and scrawl a lot of articles on Holland for the *Times* and for magazines; we go hence
in several weeks to Brussels—more articles; also to
the Ghent exposition.   We hope to be in London in
Oct. if not in N. Y. in November—*i.e.*, unless mat-

ters are materially altered. I'm sick of hotels, so is Mrs. H. of living in trunks. Any place where we anchor forever. How are you and the family! We heard your praises sung by the Naumbergs on the "Rotterdam" (by the way a splendid steamer) on the way over. Whether you will sing theirs, I can't say —as yet. Nothing new except the "Pathos" is going well in London, better in fact than N. Y. It is too high priced for one thing, for another, it came out 2 months too late; yet I shan't complain, the criticisms have been copious and fair (often severe, as they should be). I wish I had about 2 years' leisure to finish my present book (only the title page is finished), but I suppose I'll have to get back into harness soon. Damn! With regards to Mrs. Rosebault and yourself from both.

As ever,

Charles J. Rosebault.   JIM.

To Mrs. Rollins H. Wilbur

Hotel Des Pays Bas
Utrecht, Holland
Sep. 29, 1913

MY DEAR MRS. WILBUR:

Pray don't dismiss me as a hopeless correspondent or a rude one, for I've been living in Europe for a year and a half, various spots from Budapest to Berlin; just here at present after attending the opening

of the Peace Palace at The Hague. I'm sorry I won't
be able to hear your young friend play. I also hope
you are well. The last time I heard from you, you
were over in Europe. I've been writing for the *Times*
for a year (the Sunday section) on art, music, literature, etc. (no longer with the *Sun*). I must apologize for not sending you my "Pathos of Distance"—
it is because of the Distance rather than the pathos.

Sincerely, as ever,

JAMES HUNEKER.

Permanent European address: Care Brown, Shipley & Co., 123 Pall Mall, London, England.

To Charles J. Rosebault

Hotel Des Pays Bas
Utrecht, Holland
Sept. 29, 1913

DEAR KARL:

Glad to hear from you. No! we were not "Kopf
und Dochas" (as they say in Yiddish) with our
friends who crossed. I saw the lady once; my frau
spoke to her once; and I spent my spare time dodging
the young man—as I was tired, nervous and wanted
to study, and gossip of New York musicians was not
interesting in August. Thus spake Zarathustra.
Otherwise—amiable folk. I know the father, have
known him 25 years. Altogether different calibre

Why? There is something in New York atmosphere, in its moral climate that acts as a dissolvent on character. More's the pity.

Still here. Am over at Amsterdam (35 minutes away) every other day, with the great Hugo DeVries, Darwin's successor, a glorious old man of science, also with the Dutch psychiatrists and brain doctors. Preparing a good story for the *Times* on some forerunners of man. Hope to be in London in Nov. Go first to Brussels, Ghent, &c., will surely see you in N. Y. in Dec. Had a cable yesterday from Washington telling me the good news that modern art would be included on the free list tariff. Hope to get details today.

Good-bye, Auf wiedersehn. Regards to Mrs. Rosebault. (I've been accorded the honor of the "freedom" of Vienna by Dr. Weisskirchner, Burgomeister, in an elaborate document, because of that Vienna story last Spring in the *Times*.) Warum?

Also—I've just been decorated here at Utrecht with the orange (house of Orange & Nassau, you remember, royal colors), for services to art and science in Holland.

Say, Bill?

P. S. Dublin was terrible—the strike and poverty!! I've a "special" for the *Times*.

As ever,

JIM HUNEKER.

Charles J. Rosebault.

To Dr. T. C. Williams

> Hotel Des Pays Bas,
> Utrecht, Holland
> Oct. 7, 1913

[Postal Card]

DEAR DOCTOR:

We called at your house on 30th St. last July 30, but you had fled to your Maine retreat. We were over only for a few weeks; had to return to Holland for the opening of the Peace Palace at The Hague (a fine restaurant it will make some day). Now writing a study for the N. Y. *Times* (Sunday magazine) on Prof. De Vries, and his Mutation theory in Plant life. I see him every afternoon in his experimental garden up at Amsterdam (about 35 minutes from here) a great man.

> Regards from both,
> JAMES HUNEKER.

We hope to get back in Dec. Both well—and kicking! Remember us to Mrs. Williams.

> J. H.

Dr. Thomas C. Williams.

< 1914 >

To John Quinn

Westminster Court
1618 Beverly Road, Brooklyn
March 9, 1914

DEAR JOHN:

I was glad to get your letter chockful of news and pleasant—rather say consoling—words. I'm glad the Epstein head is arrived, and that the Gauguin ceiling is also here. I fancy the "Flute" will console you for the F. & A. But don't let up on A. J. He gets big money nowadays, but not too big. As you say, Lane paid him miserly prices. Thanks for your kind encouraging advice. It's all true. Yesterday we had a box at the German theatre (tip top dramatic company), lunched at Lüchow's; in the evening went to "Boris Godounow" at Metropolitan (absurd ever for you to spend money for us there, as I am persona grata), and reached home, here, late, but tired and content. Activity of all kinds is the keynote, not morbid introspection and book nosing. But my depression comes from my complaint: *i.e.*, excess of uric and the best thing is to remove the original evil, Dieting and exercise and abstinence (the last not least)! We had a lovely night at your apartment, but the ride home made us blue. Now we are in a quiet place, a beautiful view from top floor, more room and—peace. There's a pianola lurking in its covert next door, but thus far it has remained dumb. I fore-

see plenty of work here if pacific conditions continue.
I suppose you saw I had a Holland "story" in yesterday's *Times*. I hadn't the courage to read it, as
it was written in Sept. last. But it clears the way for
the London story—John, Epstein, Shaw, Anatole
France, Brandes, &c. Then I can get to work on live
topics of this humming town. Mrs. Huneker sends
regards. Next month when the air is not so nipping
and eager that invitation will be accepted with joy.
I'll drop in some day. I have good news, but prefer
to tell it in impropria persona.

As ever, sincerely,
JAMES HUNEKER.

John Quinn.

To John Quinn

Westminster Court
Brooklyn, 1618 Beverly Road
April 17, 1914

DEAR JOHN:
Thanks for your letter and the Epstein head. I'll
take it over Monday to the newspaper—perhaps
there's a chance yet for reproduction. The books
are due in the next mail. I only wanted the English
edition—as the so-called American is out of print
according to the Knopf bibliography. I want to read
their stories, then I'll fetch them to your house. The
Puck for this week, I enclose as a "sample." It's all

to be in a minor key. Edgar Saltus told me the other
day he is to be a contributor. Who knows, if the
management receives the best talent whether the thing
won't be a go? We are both distressed about your
indisposition. Don't fail to follow up treatment.
And let us give you the advice of my old Turkish
Bath rubber, who for nearly 40 years has had experience with abdominal pains in his clients. Take a
dose of castor oil; it can't hurt you! And then wait
a bit. The oil soothes and obstructions are removed.
Try it! I'm afraid you don't take enough fatty, oily
food, above all you don't drink enough liquid, but
plain water. You are too thin, John, though the
girls, I fancy, find you just right.

As ever,

John Quinn.   JAMES.

To John Quinn

Westminster Court
1618 Beverly Road
June 4, 1914

DEAR JOHN:
  Glad to hear from you. Sorry about next Saturday. It's the only time I can get with Georg Brandes
for an interview. He's hard to pin down and he
goes to Europe next week. How about Sat. 13 or 27?
Either will do if weather "permits." I hope I haven't
deranged your plans for next Saturday. I read the

proof of that *Times* article, and it would have gone in if there hadn't been a Brandes interview, and now I fear P. H. McCarthy has knocked my chances for next Sunday. However, let us hope. I'm at work on magazine articles—various sorts. The Conrad reads fairly well in typescript, but you can't tell till it's in actual type. Have just finished, for *Puck*, a diatribe against socialism, and a review of the "best" fiction of the day—American.

Dreiser leads in seriousness—but he writes clumsily. I think Hughes is a winner ("What Will People Say?"), and "The Salamander," by Owen Johnson, is a realistic study of a type known to us youths as "teasers"; indeed the author calls her plainly "a teaser." But my favorite is Katherine Fullerton Gerould—"Vain Oblations"—she is the real thing. Much art for a beginner, and more temperament, more red blood, than Edith Glacial Wharton. She has read Joseph Conrad, the new ones. But you will read later, I hope in *Puck*—and why deprive you of the displeasure in advance? Regards to El Greggo. The country is magnificent—sleep under blankets, no mosquitoes, ocean ten minutes away—all the familiar lies of the New Jersey commuter. God knows I like it, yet I prefer Holland.

Drop me a line. Thanks for the invitation.

As ever, yours,

JAMES HUNEKER.

John Quinn.

To Rupert Hughes

1618 Beverly Road
Brooklyn, N. Y.
Aug. 11, 1914

[Postal]

LIEBER RUPERTO:

Just a line to say that I'm *not* to blame for the bad break on my article on Jos. Conrad in the Aug. *North American Review.* The name of H. G. Wells was dropped out in the types, though it is in my MS. I haven't reached the senile state when I would credit "The Island of Dr. Moreau" to Kipling! But it reads that way. I hope you will look at the story; you will see I admire a different Conrad from "Chance."

As ever,

JIM H.

Rupert Hughes.

To John Quinn

1618 Beverly Road, Brooklyn
August 31st, 1914

DEAR JOHN:

Enclosed MS. The reason I didn't send it to you before is that Harpers asked me to take out twelve lines, too long for a page. I did so. When the story was printed, I put them back for my book. They are not important. I have marked them—end of Part 1, end of Part 2, chiefly quotations. I've also included in the general study, not only the account of my visit to J. C. in 1912,—as a pendant—but also part of that *Puck* notice of "Chance," the latter written before the *North American Review* article. So much for Conrad. I'll speak again of the accursed error. But I am childish at times, despite my teeth. Thanks for your words of consolation. They were very consoling. The Missus begs to be remembered. I am through with all work until September 21.

Can't write—only sneeze. Then I'll be in fettle; not an ounce of uric in my skin.

The *Times* printed (much excised) my "Coney Island" story today. It stinks, like the subject.

As ever,

Jim.

John Quinn.

To Mrs. Charles H. Ditson

Westminster Court
1618 Beverly Road
Brooklyn, N. Y.
Nov. 16, 1914

Dear Mrs. Ditson:

It was good to hear from you again. Living out here in Flatbush among baby-carriages, cemeteries and never ending funerals (not to mention the lovely

air, view of the park, and low rental!) we had resigned ourselves to the inevitable—in Brooklyn even
Alexander Lambert would be lost. Will you tell
Mr. Ditson I'm very much obliged *in re* the music.
Mr. Strauss—who is now my present employer on
Puck, Nathan Strauss—is very musical and a power
in the newspaper world. As to the War. It's a bore;
besides, as Stendhal says, it interrupts conversation.
However, as it promises to drive out the dancing
craze, supplanting it with the knitting neurosis, I
suppose it has its uses. Seriously, my dear lady,
don't read the newspapers; not even the headlines.
(I made an exception today when Bernard Shaw's
article—a wonder!—appeared in the Sunday *Times.*)
But think of music; of the Altman collection; of
Bauer's lovely Brahms playing. I've finished 2 new
books this summer, cursing all the while my poverty,
and the waste of millions. Another atrocity! No
pilsner beer from Bohemia, who is to blame! England, of course. White, red, blue, orange papers!
So many Seidlitz powders. *No,* don't think of war.
Be a Christian Scientist (humbug) for the nonce.
There is no war! and then there isn't, for the believer.
Alas! if it were but so. La pauvre Belgique! Love-
liest of little countries! Our regards to you both.

As ever,
JAMES HUNEKER.

Mrs. Charles H. Ditson.

To Rupert Hughes

1618 Beverly Road, Brooklyn
June 4, 1915

DEAR RUPERT:

Thank you for "Empty Pockets," but my pockets
will be empty if I get any more such stories, for I
neglected my work altogether yesterday, reading till
12:40 a. m., and went to bed in a rage, because from
sheer ocular fatigue I was forced to close the book at
½ p. 528. It seems to me you are taking up my challenge about New York novel. I smell Dostoievsky
and Hughes in the handling of the East Side episodes.
A corker, Rupert! The other novel—last year—is
less episodical, *èlan Schwung.* It ought to be a
"seller." You, too, I note, indulge in the route elliptical. Very effective, too, is your "retrospect." All
this in confidence. I'll write about it later.

As ever,

JIM.

Rupert Hughes.

To John Quinn

1618 Beverly Road, Brooklyn
July 14, 1915

DEAR JOHN:

Thanks for your letter; thanks for the offer of the
Conrad book—I'd like to read it, though I fear its

inclusion is problematical; I've read page proof of the J. C. chapter, which is the first. But I'll do what I can. Thanks, also, *in re*: the Corbin-Calumet Co. *Puck* has changed printers; in the muddle attendant upon "copy" being shifted my story was left in the lurch; but it is announced on the cover. Next week it will appear as usual. July 26th there is announced a special book review issue. The Brooklyn story cost me more trouble than it was worth. But did you see the pages devoted to Joseffy in the *Times*—magazine section—last Sunday a week ago? It came from my heart, written in hot haste as it was. In "Iconoclasts" (1905) I printed for the first time the real name of Gabriele D'Annunzio, *i.e.*, Gaetano Rapagnetto. Yeats is by far too young— all of a sudden; he knew George when his hair was russet, and his grouping is, to say the least, slightly prejudiced. G. M. is a great literary artist, whatever else he may be; to put him in with the other two—fudge. Did you see yesterday's funny story about Cronley in the *Times*. Too bad about any artist who goes into this accursed war. Glad we are you enjoyed the visit. "Do it" again. Reading proof spells disillusionment. I dislike my new book heartily. Don't read the article on Jules Laforge in the *N. A. Review*—it's cut. Otherwise nothing new. I'm going tomorrow morning to Holland-American Line to see John McFadden off on the *Rotterdam*. I begged him not to go, not because of bomb or torpedoes, but because of the unsettled condition of England, but his son is at the front in France, and I fancy both Mrs. McFadden and John H. are going over on his account. But I hate like hell to see them go. "A bientot John!"

As ever,
JIM HUNEKER.

John Quinn.

To E. P. Mitchell

1618 Beverly Road,
Brooklyn, N. Y.
Sept. 11, 1915

MY DEAR MR. MITCHELL:

Because I fear you may see the enclosed before I send it to you, I wish to explain to you that it is a chapter in my Souvenirs, rather, *Avowals* now appearing daily (week days) in the Philadelphia *Press* (Rodman Wanamaker's paper). Alas! I have reached the age of anecdotage; nevertheless, I wrote with a pen 185,000 words from May 15 to Aug. 20, last. The series is to run till Nov. 9. A big job for an elderly party. If I sound boastful about the work I did while with the *Sun*—and it was all of 15 years—and with your kindly co-operation—it is because I am proud to have had the opportunity, prouder still to have had the friendship of Edward Page Mitchell. When book form is achieved I shall give myself the pleasure of sending you a copy. I'm in the throes of hay-fever, but hope to get away by the end of the month—probably Atlantic City. With best wishes from Mrs. Huneker and myself to you and yours, I am as ever.

Sincerely,
JAMES GIBBONS HUNEKER.

E. P. Mitchell.

To Benjamin De Casseres

1618 Beverly Road
Brooklyn, N. Y.
Oct. 24, 1915

DEAR BEN:

At last you are between covers! Thank you for the copy and the inscription. Some of the verse (very much libre! is familiar. The volume seems to represent your revolt period. Later I hope to see some rhythmic prose "easy, ironical, gay," your present serene mood of indifference is the best front to turn to the world. *Don't* answer any of the forthcoming reviews—that is, unless you like a shindy; and notoriety! I've asked S. & S. to send you my new cargo of putrid sea and land food.

As ever cordially,
JAMES HUNEKER.

Benjamin De Casseres.

To Richard Aldrich

1618 Beverly Road, Brooklyn
Nov. 9, 1915

DEAR RICHARD:

I wish to thank you for that gracious reference to the programme-band in last Sunday's *Times*. I agree with you absolutely as to the disputed authorship, but I had to "follow copy" (the piece in itself is pretty and ingratiating). Vol. 1 of the Schirmer edition of piano classics, edited by Louis Oesterle, is temporarily out of print or stock, so I couldn't read your preface (presuming you wrote one to that particular volume as you did to the others). Did you say anything of the Rossi piece? And if not why was it included in the list as genuine? G. got it from this volume, he told me. I'm puzzled. Drop me a line here at your leisure. Dick—may God have mercy on your soul, is my wish at the beginning of this tremendous musical season.

As ever cordially,
JAMES HUNEKER

Richard Aldrich.

P. S.   Doesn't H. E. K. look fit as a fiddle?

Photo by Applegate, Phila.

JAMES HUNEKER (at right)

From a photograph taken with some old friends in Philadelphia

< 1916 >

To H. L. Mencken

1618 Beverly Road, Brooklyn
Jan. 18/16

DEAR H. L.:

I'm shaky today with a bad cold and slight fever contracted at the private rehearsal of the Russian Ballet last Sunday night. "Dr." Huneker—Mevrouw—thinks I'm better off if I don't go out and I think so, too; but I hate to give up that luncheon engagement, and I'm writing to say so now. Too bad! I'm seldom sick, yet this is the second time within 3 months I've begged off. Next time I'll go even if I shiver—as I'm doing now.

I'm afraid of grip—so let it go at that!

Hope to see you soon, and with Nathan. Regards and regrets.

Yours cordially,
JIM HUNEKER.

H. L. Mencken.

To H. L. Mencken

1618 Beverly Road
Brooklyn, N. Y. (U. S.?)
Mar. 20/16

DEAR H. L.:

Greetings from one who escaped the dread portals! I was all in Feb. 29th but escaped for a little while.

Pneumonia, &c., weak, sitting up, hopeful. I write to say that I should like very much to sell *S. S.* a story (the "Supreme Sin" got into the March *Forum!*) I have the following books to deliver—and I need all the cash I can get, for sickness is a luxury:—a 4,000 words, entitled:

1. "Venus or Valkyr"—a frivolous, low-brow story located at Bayreuth. Purely musical environment but tale is the pursuit of two girls by a New York swell.

2. A Jewish musical story, "Crucified," about 2,500 words. Praised in MS. by Zangwill. Original title, "Eloi, Eloi, Lama Sahavthani." (No good—too recondite.) Motive—the inability to escape writing Hebraic music, though he tries to write Christian. Hence "Crucified." It's novel and full of local color—(Jewish).

3. A morbid tale, "A Modern Montsalvat," a crack at "Parsifal" and the will to renounce. 2,500 words. Very sombre.

4. A showing up of S. Wagner. Title, "A Tragic Sentimentalist." Fiction, 3,000 words. Hard words.

May I send you, say, "Venus or Valkyr" and the Jewish story? Drop me a line. We must foregather in May. I'll be uncaged by then.

As ever,

JAMES HUNEKER.

H. L. Mencken.

To H. L. Mencken

1618 Beverly Road
Brooklyn, April 13/16

DEAR SON:

Glad you survived the egotistical dose. By all means let me read MS. of the chapter. Glad you liked "Melo"; yet I think there are better stories in "Visionaries": to wit: "The Eighth Deadly Sin," "Rebels of the Moon," "The Third Kingdom," "The Mock Sun" (really an intimate study of Maeterlinck *chez lui*) (this in confidence, for "Moritz" is a nice chap and his slim volume of one act plays will outlive all his philosophy *à la* Emerson and Von Hartmann), not forgetting "The Eternal Dual" and, of course, "Aholibah." Just because I believe you haven't seen these tales, I've asked Scribner's to send you a copy of them; if you have a copy give the new one away. You are right, the Mahler is a big work; but Phila. produced it first—see the hole in the critical millstone.

There are lots of things I want to talk over with you, my boy—not my tiresome stuff—but Dreiser, Morris, Fuller, Henry James, &c. Let us meet in May or early in June and, for the love of literature let us dawdle over our cups. That damnable 5:26 for Washington always interrupts conversation.

Regards, as ever JAMES THE PENMAN,

(who wishes he could dictate or play the type keys)

H. L. Mencken.

To H. L. Mencken

1618 Beverly Road
Brooklyn, April 24/16

MY DEAR MENCKEN:

Pardon my silence. I've a bad cold again, but this time only in my head. Hope to get rid of it if the sun shines again. The William Sunday's tracts were edifying though I should have preferred several of his collections! What a shrewd chap! Enclosed is only one of several that have come my way. I felt assured after reading my "obituary" (as they call it in Phila.) *you* would come in for some hard knocks. Your name is as suspicious as mine—and then Nietzsche! What a lark! "The Menckens, Nathans, Vierecks"—why George? I'm blocking out the story. It's for *S. S.* not later than Jan., 1917. I want it to land in a volume of short stories. (Sold "The Husband of Madame" to *Scribner's Magazine*— $150. I'll chortle as R. L. S. once remarked.) Scene Met. Opera House. Time—last decade 19th century, with today's singers. Title, a beauty of a title. Save it for your ear; and it was no joke when I wrote that I have my first *par.* and last sentence. The filling in will be done this summer and fall. About 6 chapters fiction and fornications, not too much psychologizing. My model is to be the absolute reverse of "Evelyn Innes" for my heroine is a real woman, not a lady studio figure.

Don't send back clipping.   Hope to meet you and
George when the Bock flows next month.

Cordially,
JAMES HUNEKER.

To H. L. Mencken

1618 Beverly Road
Brooklyn, May 2/16

MY DEAR MENCKEN:

Those Sunday cards, etc., are marvellous "human
documents." What mean souls (?) there are to be
saved in this slough of sin!   I studied with Georges
Mathias—who told me much of his master, Chopin;
also a few lessons with Theodore Ritter—who used
his mother's family name; hence he is listed under
his real name as a Liszt pupil.   I never saw L. at
Weimar but I think (?) I saw him once in Paris in
1878.   Perhaps if I had gone to Weimar I shouldn't
have written that peculiarly putrid "Life."   Adelaide
Neilson played here in 1877.   She gave me my first
genuine feeling—not—!—!   Enclosed shows the in-
fluence of your article.   Now they are all "claiming"
me since you sowed the seed.   I hope N— will come
out in better shape.   Let us say the weeks of May 15,
or 22nd.   I'm busy this and next week getting hold
of myself.   I don't last!   My thirst is slim—bad
sign.   More power to your pen.

Greetings from

H. L. Meneken.   J. H.

To E. P. Mitchell

1618 Beverly Road
Brooklyn, Aug. 27, 1916

MY DEAR MR. MITCHELL:

I had hoped the enclosed would be printed ahead of the other papers, but the *Times* in its literary supplement had a page this morning devoted to the new G. Moore book.* However, it didn't dwell on the chief and most interesting quality of the life of Christ. I have and I hope it won't be curtailed or "edited," as I've given no offence to the orthodox and I've kept the story within bounds—about 2,000 words. Naturally, I'll sign it if you see fit, as I am quite willing to stand for what I write. If the writing is too crabbed or cryptic for the proofreader I'll gladly correct the galleys and return at once as I'm anxious not to play 3rd fiddle to any other reviewer, and my story is less a review than a study of the psychologic characteristics of Moore and of his puppets. I'll give myself the pleasure of calling on you next Tuesday before 12 noon. We go to Cuba on Saturday. Hoping you enjoyed your vacation, I am as ever,

JAMES HUNEKER.

Edward P. Mitchell.

* "The Brook Kerith," by George Moore.

1917 〉

To Alden March

1618 Beverly Road
Brooklyn, N. Y.
Jan. 5/17

MY DEAR ALDEN:

Thank you for your greeting. We wish you and yours a new year without too many tribulations; for to wish happiness to any mortal—even I. W. W.—would be to invite the petty jealousy of the gods. Pray say to Richard and Magers that I wish them joy—at stated intervals, of course (Luther advised moderation: 2 times weekly, im jahr 104 mal!). Also that I hope to join knees with all of the members of the Independent Order of Tapeworms (Ltd.) on April 15th, at 1 p. m.; that being the first free day— I think—for this hard driven pen. (The pen—is— mightier than the sword; aphorism from the Golden Treasury of Princeton by Peck's Bad Boy). Charley Hart drops in at intervals to tell a consoling anecdote. Billy Chase says that my Phila. work in 1917 "was a gentleman's job" compared with the present one—2 tons of coal a day to put in. Mr. Ochs is particularly nice to me. Your name is often pronounced. The Sunday Mag. is once more on view. Hurry back, Alden; I'll be glad to do anything for you from pitch and toss to obituaries. Regards from my Missus.

As ever,

Alden March.   JIM.

To Mme. Frida Ashforth

1618 Beverly Road
Brooklyn, Mar. 4/17

You naughty girl Frida!

I wouldn't trust you even at 76 (and I think you
are exaggerating your age on purpose) if a handsome
young chap eloped with you!

Thanks for the anecdotes; all new to me and side-
splitting. With love from both.

As ever, I am your devoted "young" (?) friend,

JAMES HUNEKER.

Mme. Frida Ashforth.

To E. C. Marsh

Westminster Court
1618 Beverly Road
Brooklyn, May 17/17

DEAR MARSH:

Thank you for the "Swinburne." From cover to
cover it's wholly admirable; tactful, sympathetic,
critical. I shall make a quotation from it in my new
book. I once saw and spoke to S. He was an ap-
parition. When Paderewski came here in '91 he
looked like the Watts "Swinburne" (I mean the
painter, not the egregious jailer Watts-Dunton of
Putney). So much so that Burne-Jones made a
sketch that is a dazzling double of Algernon (who

boozed and whored, but was a normal male; that's
the reason he so detested Oscar of the Wilde clan).

Hope to see you before you go to your summer
yacht. I am absolutely without work; hence my
Steinway Grand wakes the echoes of Flatbush and
Greenwood Cemetery. Again thanks, and greetings
from

JAMES HUNEKER.

E. C. Marsh.

To H. L. Mencken

Wed., July 25/17

DEAR HAL:

Up at Stamford last Saturday evening. I read that
most eloquent and highly flattering story in the *Evening Mail*. Naturally I crook my knee and doff my
bonnet (and did you note the sour haughty look on
my mug?) The *coda* was particularly saddening;
alas! I can't live on my books, and now not on my
articles—I've sold nothing since last April 15th (*Sun*)
except the De Gourmont article in *N. A. Review*
(June) sadly clipped on account of space exigencies.
I'm hoping you will bull my market. But whether
you do or you don't I'm obliged to you for one more
courtesy. The *S. S.* is a corker this month. I'm not
well. Reading proof.

As ever,

H. L. Mencken.   JIM.

To H. L. Mencken

1618 Beverly Road
Oct. 11/17

DEAR HAL:

Thank you for your praise. The book is admittedly in the vein popular; *Puck* harnessed to the *Sun* and *Times*. Heavy going at times—nevertheless. I read "Pistols for Two" on my return with joy. It is simply fiendish in conception and witty in execution. Two noble kinsmen and their obituaries! Who is "Rycker?" I find his name on the "blurb" of "Hunicorns" (as Brander Matthews has re-christened the book) and no one at Scribner's seems to know how such a name came. I'll utilize the shop for a short story—a Frankenstein thrust on me. (Casimir Rycker born Moldavia 1900; burnt alive for the unpardonable crime of raping his divorced wife's mother and writing a brochure on the noble art of miscegenation.) How's that? I'm up to my dandruff in work; a rush job, over Nov. 15. But then I'll lay off for a month, and meet you anywhere in *Michelobia*—Heard from George.

As ever,

JIM.

H. L. Mencken.

To John Quinn

1618 Beverly Road, N. Y.
Oct. 30, 1917

MY DEAR JOHN:

Your very kind letter is welcome. Unhappily we are only at the beginning of settling down. I am away every Friday and usually Sat. of each week in Philadelphia, where I am writing the musical critique for all important events; symphony concerts, opera, recitals. It's hard luck to get into harness at my age after just 15 years' escape, but what am I to do? Here, if I take a job as music critic it means slavery for 7 days in the week and not more than 50 plunks. With a 50th part of the work I can earn more. The trip is easy. The art club is comfortable. The work is not terrible. The Philadelphia cuisine a joy. So there you are. I saw the *Times* editorial with the mention of your name. Hurrah! The "Eminent" is absolutely true, and only fitting that you should be so called. I also read the London letter in the *Art News'* current issue and see that you have got two great Epsteins. Bully news. Epstein, like Brancusi, is worth an article. He is one of the advanced Sculptors who is able in his research for pure form to evade the grotesque. What a hell of a fuss they are raising over Barnard's "Lincoln." Not a word, though, as to its artistic merit. Only whether it's a portrait. God! what Philistines we are! (I haven't

seen the Barnard work, and I remember the Balzac-
Rodin—controversy.) And the R—— marriage.
Funeral baked meats, &c. A divorced woman, too.
Oh the Holy, Holy wholly material Church.

Regards from both. Hope to arrange a night here
as soon as we shake down. Vote for Mitchell, John.
I shall.

As ever,

JIM.

John Quinn.

To Havelock Ellis

1618 Beverly Road
Brooklyn, N. Y., U. S. A.
Dec. 23, 1917

MY DEAR MR. ELLIS:

I am glad, indeed, to hear from you. I often
think of you and the day dear Arthur Symons brought
me to your "den"—a memorable day for me. All
your books I re-read, and "Impressions and Comments" I have by me every night; it contains the
quintessence of Ellis, of the philosophy and poetry
and a general attitude to life that is for me so consoling in the midst of vulgarity, triviality and terror.
You are the English Montaigne, plus a science he
never dreamed of. I am both sorry and glad to
learn you have left Cornwall for London. The sea is
the great consolatrix—sea and sky. I wrote at once

to you when the cable told us the sad news; perhaps the letter never reached Carfin. I had met Mrs. Ellis here. We talked of you, she worshipped you. A glorious intelligence, hers, and a noble woman. Pardon me, dear old friend, if I awaken painful memories. My wife and I sympathize with you—no mere lip-service this. It's splendid news to hear that Arthur is himself again. I'm now reading his "Tristam" which he had read to me from MS. at Lauderdale Mansions in 1903. I hope he is happy. Mrs. Huneker and I met him at a concert—De Pachmann, the Chopinzee I think it was—in the spring of 1913.

He looked rather ill then. And you, are you in your usual form now? I hope so. Need I tell you that nothing is selling here but war books—which is as it should be; but it's pretty hard on Journalists of my sort who can only write of the Seven Arts. I had a lovely letter from Maurice Maeterlinck the other day. He is at Nice.

When shall we 3 meet again?

With heartiest regards—and a moiety of adieux for Arthur. I am, my dear sir,

Cordially yours,

JAMES HUNEKER.

Havelock Ellis.

< 1918 >

To H. L. Mencken

N. Y., Jan. 13, 1918

[Postal]

Thanks for quotations on stock market, but it's my belief you are rigging the book market. They ought to be my posthumous prices! "Going up" and so am I if hard times last. Fishless Fridays will soon be followed by Beerless Booze days. But I'm sitting on my Quaker City job, cold and all, and only longing for Spring and more coal.

As ever,

H. L. Mencken. J. H.

To H. E. Krehbiel

1618 Beverly Road, Brooklyn, N. Y.
(though it really isn't, not by a dam sight)
Jan. 19, 1918

DEAR HARRY:

On arriving from the city of Terrapin and fried oysters this morning (2nd, Brahms and Berlioz Damnation excerpts yesterday symphony concert over there) I found your welcome letter. I hope enclosed won't reach you too late. Please return at leisure. It's the only copy I have and I keep it only for reference. I'm not responsible for proofreading. I never see copy in Phila.

Don't be cast down! You are playing in luck. What! South just now when we are supping sorrow

and Garfield tea with a long spoon. Go to! I envy
you and hope to see you on the Avenue in the early
Spring. No more opera in Phila. this season. I'm
getting ready for the bread line. I particularly enjoyed your footnote to musical history in the
Tribune last Sunday week. Oh Gee! what a wallop!
With regards to Mrs. Krehbiel from both and to you,
sir, I am as ever,

JIM.

(Poor Von Inten has gone. Another.)

H. E. Krehbiel.

To Frank J. Wilstach

1618 Beverly Road
Brooklyn, N. Y.
Jan. 21, 1918

DEAR FRANK:

Thank you for your pleasing words; but where
did you get the notion that I plumed myself on proofreading? Was I ever imbecile enough to brag of
what I can't do, *i.e.* read proof, or write a legible
hand? None of my books—mosaics, not real books
except 2 or 3—are proof read with care. I am an
abominable proof hound, being too hasty and suffering from that mental and physical (the same
thing) nausea, best described in the Scriptures—the
dog that returneth to its vomit. I loathe what I have
written—truly disjecta membra—dead fecal matter,
of me—as Walt would say.

Here are a few similes that prove of service to you.
George Moore: "Esther Waters" (revised edition,
Brentano, page 1):
"and the lamplight made the curious curves of a beautiful ear look like a piece of illuminated porcelain."
Ibid. "In these moments all fear that he would
one day desert died away like an ugly wind" (p. 195).
Ibid. "The thick hair that used to encircle her
pale prominent temples like rich velvet, looked now
like a black silk band frayed and whitened at the
seam."

John Galsworthy: "The Dark Flower" (p. 14):

"It was so jolly to watch the mountains lying in
this early light like huge beasts."

There are some more which, when I have time I'll
send you. The Deaker is bully prose, pungent prose.

Cordially,

Frank J. Wilstach.   JIM HUNEKER.

To Mme. Frida Ashforth

Westminster Court
1618 Beverly Road, Brooklyn
April 10, 1918

MY DEAR FRIDA:
I arrived from Phila. early this morning—3:30
a. m. on the Operatic Special and went to bed in a bad

humor—the futility of travelling 200 miles in an afternoon and evening to hear that droning "Samson et Dalila!"—and at 8 a. m. I was too nervous to sleep, arose, drank a cup of tea, and still was in a bad humor. Then the post brought your letter and my irritability vanished. No wonder! You are royally responsive to my request and again your debtor—as I have been for 30 years in matters vocal. Of course *you* know *you* know it all—don't butter polite phrases about my ignorance, or even about Henderson—who, however, has forgotten more about singing—I mean as a critic, not as a teacher—than all his colleagues. Your letter proves my assertion. With a few words it sums up the Galli Curci complex. All obscure technical points are clear now. I thank you. You are a dear, as well as a good girl. What you say about "brains, brains, brains," should be framed and hung in every singing teacher's studio; also in every critic's memory. And Lucy Gates! I thought my memory didn't fail me. As soon as the Phila. job is through, early in May, we shall pay Frida Ashford a formal visit. If I write of Galli I shall most certainly quote you, even if briefly. It's all nonsense for you to hide your light under a bushel. Considering the magnitude of the blaze and its persistent brilliancy through so many years. Again thanks, Frida. I humbly sign myself a contemporary!

As ever,

Mme. Frida Ashforth.   Jim.

To Mme. Frida Ashforth

Westminster Court
1618 Beverly Road, Brooklyn
April 13, 1918

DEAR FRIDA:

I didn't know that the little Breslau was one of your flock!   Good heavens, she is the most promising of the new generation—voice, temperament and musical horse-sense.   Whenever she sings I write well of her, and all this without knowing her artistic ancestry. "Shanewis" is simply comic opera spoiled by an attempt at the tragic in Act II.   The music does not rise above the level of Tosti's drawing room mawkish song tunes.   The orchestration, like the curate's egg is good in spots, but it's all borrowed, effect upon effect.   Cadman writes pleasantly for the voice; that's all.   The libretto is silly.   De Koven can beat this music hands down.   Breslau is the best thing in the show.   But the mediocrity of it all!   If this is good American music, what is bad?   Jesus! All this entre nous.

With love,

JIM.

Mme. Frida Ashforth.

To John Quinn

1618 Beverly Road, Brooklyn
Sunday, April 21/18

MY DEAR JOHN:

It was with joy we read of your return to health—
and hard work. I've only just had a chance to answer
your welcome letter, as I spent the week, with
the exception of one day, in Phila. I felt, when I
read your letter from the hospital, that you were not
yet fit to dissipate your nervous energies in writing,
so I was rude enough in good faith, to bid you rest.
But, thank the gods on whose treacherous laps lie our
individual destinies, you are soon to become your old
self again, with that inescapable nuance of profound
experience caused by intense suffering. When we
meet, which will be soon—for my season is expiring
early in May—you must tell me precisely what your
medical man would call the "history of the case." It
will be of tremendous interest to me. Phila. is
charming after the horrors of noisy, crowded N. Y. I
now am a member of the Art Club. We may go over
to live there in the autumn. But I'll tell you all about
it next month. We can first lunch and then you must
come down here. Josephine sends her regards and
congratulations. This sounds as if you are going to
be married. Perhaps you are. I haven't heard any
rumor to that effect, but I think matrimony is about
due for you; you have reached the age of unreason

and there are plenty of nice women who would make
your later years (ah! they will soon come, John)
happy; if not happy, then contented. Take the fatal
leap, my boy! I know several girls that would be
happy. So do you. I like *one* of them. So do
you. Jump, John, jump, and to hell with the hind-
most—as we used to say down Donegal way. (But
don't blame me if the job proves a botched one.
Thus do I "hedge" my advice.) Hurray for hell!
I'm in better spirits than in 1917. Perhaps the world
will be free of the incubus of war by 1919; anyhow,
by 1922!

As ever,

John Quinn.   JIM.

To John Quinn

1618 Beverly Road, Brooklyn
May 14, 1918

MY DEAR JOHN:

Your letter with its description of your terrifying
experience is a masterpiece. I literally shuddered
over it. So did Jozia. However, you are better,
though it will be at least a year before you will be as
strong as your old self. The Phila. booklet is a bore.
It is as dry as—hell. But I had to write it. It is now
on sale, thanks to newspaper publicity. Did I tell
you McCloy is managing editor of Phila. *Telegraph*—
thanks to my recommendation. He is more than
making good. A strong adjunct to the staff, I hear.

Enclosed—sent me by Mencken—shows that other cities besides Chicago, &c. Also here in New York city. But where does the poor devil of an author come in? Listen, John: My books bring me a derisive income. I'm offered the music criticism dept. of the *Times* (N. Y.). I can't take it because I'm not strong enough. I was born 1860, so I'm past 58. The life is too exhausting—5 or 6 concerts daily and the opera every night. You write and write and write—nibblings, nothing of moment. No, I'll go over to Phila. rather, and permanently. Good offer, little work—nice city. I'm a member now of the Art Club, one of the best in town. The contract is ready—farewell to old N. Y. after 32 years! It is rather disheartening. In the interim I've signed contract for serial rights of a long projected book—or books, with Rodman Wanamaker and the *Press* (Alden March), 200,000 words. Every day—for 1,000 words 6 times a week are to appear daily. (No Sunday stuff.) The job is appalling, ranging as it will over 50 years' experience. But it pays. There is the leveler of all effort, artistic or otherwise. When I get afloat I'll make the engagement with your approbation and we shall meet then and I shall explain. I saw a perfectly ripping Picasso at the Independent Show. Davies says it is yours. If so, congratulations; that belly is exquisite. Love from both.

As ever,

John Quinn.   JIM.

To Richard Bach

1618 Beverly Road
Brooklyn, N. Y.
June 30, 1918

RICHARD BACH:

Was that dialogue for a comedy? If you wish I'll stop the scenes now (and damn glad to do it, as hot weather is here and I'm getting lazy). Tell Mrs. Beamish I've expurged the scandals (the only viable part of my memories). But, with your permission, and her acquiescence, I shall relate as many as she can endorse when we reunite in the autumn.

Thanks, all the same, my lad, for your letter. It made me smile over here in drab Flatbush.

With cordial regards,
JAMES HUNEKER.
Richard Cœur de Lion Beamisch.

To Richard Bach

July 14, 1918 (Vive la France!)

DEAR DICK:

I can't answer letters till Sunday, so pardon delay in answering yours with enclosed. Thanks. I'm glad A. M. is taking a rest. I hope you and yours are well. Regards from house to house.

I'm correcting section stuff to be mailed to you tomorrow, 92,000 words to date—only 100,000 more. I begin to see daylight. But my hand is shaky. I note with frozen wrath that last Tuesday *Shool* (a synagogue) was spelt "School"—although I corrected it in proof; and to add injury to insult they put the school in quotes—Boches! However, don't bother White and his staff. They are working wonders. Only—if they wouldn't "correct" my copy after I pass on it—I caught "Georges" Sand just in time, a natural enough error; but *she* wrote it "George"; it was her pen name. Oh to see you, drink with you, and say—the war (of words) is over!

As ever,

Richard Bach   SHAMUS BACH.
(Richard Beamish).

To Mrs. Samuel W. Moore

1618 Beverly Road
Brooklyn, N. Y.
July 14, 1918

MY DEAR AUNT AUBIE:
(We cabled you that 40 years ago.)

Your letter kindly forwarded by Mr. Presser or Mr. Cooke gave me great pleasure. And pleased too, am I to learn that dear old "Sam" (the old names are the best, because real!) still writes to you and Uncle George—he lives. What vitality is yours! Your father (Joseph Janvier Woodward, thanks for the cor.rection, my memory is treacherous) was another vital man. His second wife sat on his venerable knees in the window of the 2nd story Race St. house. The spectacle amused my own father, who called the lady the "red-haired tabby." But you at 76—it's impossible, dear old friend. (You got my age—59 next Jan. 31st, 1919.) What an artistic foreground you have had. We left America forever in 1912, settled in Holland (Utrecht) and to return in 1914—l'année fatal! May return to Phila. to die there. When my book of "avowals" is published (when?) I'll send you a copy with the errors regarding you and yours eliminated. Do you wish to read any of my later critical books (Egoists, 1909); (Promenades, 1910); (Franz Liszt)—not much of a biography—1911; (The Pathos of Distance, 1913); (New Cosmopolis, 1915); (Ivory Apes and Peacocks, 1915); (Unicorns, 1917). Say the word and I'll send any one or all with love and admiration for a great artistic soul—yours!

Yours,
JAMES HUNEKER.

Mrs. Samuel Woodward Moore.

To Mme. Frida Ashforth

1618 Beverly Road
Brooklyn, N. Y.
Aug. 11, 1918

MY DEAR FRIDA:

Thank you for your kind and informing letter. I shall, if you have no objections, use the graphic picture you present of the Patti household. I knew Antonio but he was getting old. We drank *Strega* cordial at *Buchmagui's* on 3rd Ave., near 14th st. He had married a girl younger than himself, hence the *Strega*. She broke his back, so his loving nephew Alfredo told me. Aunt Carlotta lived with Theodore Ritter in Paris. I'm still at it, hot or cold. Have written 140,000 words. Hope to end in late Sept. There is a possibility of our going to Phila. to end my days. (I'll be 59 in Jan., 1919) as I have a fair offer from the *Press*. But it will be pulling teeth to leave N. Y. Even Flatbush is nearer the Bowery than Phila. And I've been here since 1886; left Phila. 1878; while Jozia is born in N. Y. So we sadly contemplate the change; but what to do! The war has killed my business; newspapers and magazines want *only* war news or stories. Let me whisper a secret in your ear. The N. Y. *Times* has asked me to take charge of the musical department. But I fear it would use me up —many concerts a day, opera every night; even with an assistant!—I'm not so spry as I was. Last season the Phila. job was comparatively easy—twice a week! However, "Needs must when the devil drives." I'll take what I get and be glad of anything in these trying times. Four years of outgo, and no fixed income, phew! It's knocked my never corpulent bank account into a skeleton!

But I'm not a man easily beaten, and with health and a pen I'll pull through. Hard-luck stories are

MADONNA BY HANS HOLBEIN

Impeccable Holbein!

No evasive handling; yet the human soul in all its subtlety shines forth
from these solidly modelled countenances; no capering chromatics distract
the attention from the few large tones soberly soldered one to the other.
Humanity here, in all its breadth, simplicity and sincerity, is not to be
doubted. The poet speaks, Der dichter spricht, but also the painter
enamored of surfaces and sentiment.

(Commentary by James Huneker)

not interesting, so pardon this little wail of woe! Only
—I don't like moving.   I belong to one of the best
clubs over in Phila. and my brother lives there, and
I have many friends; still. Don't bother answering this.   I'll send you the page when it appears
which contains the account of your doings; also an
earlier article in which poor Albert Steinberg (whose
name was really Abraham) and his sad cremation.
You and Theodore Stein were his only friends.   With
love from both.   As ever,

                                             JIM.

  - Yours for cooler weather.
Mme. Frida Ashforth.

To John Quinn

Westminster Court
Aug. 25/18

MY DEAR JOHN:
   Will it be too much trouble to re-tell me that Oscar
Wilde-George Moore anecdote?   I've mislaid your
letter with it.   I mean the one about Oscar who said
he knew George too well; that was the reason he never
spoke to him—something of the sort; but I would like
the exact phrases.   Don't curse me for my careless
sieve of a memory!   I'm all in but over the top by
Sept. 1st; about 175,000 words since May 15.   And
no padding, space filling words. The stuff appears
regularly.

We hope you are having a pleasant summer. We are not. The Phila. matter is still *in ubibus*. I'm trying to dodge going over. After 33 years here off and on—well, you know how hard it would be to retire to backwaters, even if Hog Island is making all the country hum. Let me hear from you this week some time and I'll call you blest. Regards and love from both. As ever,

JAMES.

John Quinn.

To Alden March

1618 Beverly Road:
Brooklyn, N. Y.
Sep. 4/18

MY DEAR ALDEN:

I am sick. Hay-fever. My head is a blazing hell and my nose is running like a soap-boiler's a . . . in war-time. The Missus has had no servant since a month. She, too, is worn-out. We should like very much to go away. But we lack the cash. I think Atlantic City will be a good spot to sneeze in. The White Mts. are too far away. I'll be near my proof —and only one hour from the *Press*. We wish to go toward end of next week. Now, couldn't you persuade the treasury to unloose $500 before then! The last cheque of $200 that you personally sent me paid me in full till August 24th on a Saturday. So if you sent me $500 it would pay me in full till next Sept. 28th; also Saturday; that would leave only another $500 due Sat. Nov. 9th, when our contract of 5 months (22 weeks) expires. Last Thursday, Aug. 29th, I went over the Top and wrote Finis to 184,000 words. Your Mr. White of the *Press* composing-room carefully estimated 430 words to my writing page, and I've written 422 pages—I have 43 still to send you soon; 18,500 words; and the dessert of the verbal banquet. As there are 133 days in our con-tract—at 1,000 words a day—that allows about 50,000 words for you to play with; but your editions have been generous, printing some days as high as 1,500 and 2,000 words. However, it's none of my affair, as I readily understand the exigencies of "make-up," etc. The main thing is that I shall expect my pound of flesh nominated in the bond, whether you finish the story Oct. 9th or Nov. 9th. I go into this intricate figuration to show you that you have plenty of security for the advance $500, which I so urgently need. We can't get away without it, Alden; so please do me the favor as speedily as you can. You might run down and take dinner with us at At-lantic City; better still, bring the mysterious and hitherto invisible Mrs. Alden March with you. Mrs. Huneker has asked not once, but ten times, why she hasn't met her. We suspect you have her immured! Ah! these jealous husbands and in 1918! I'm put-ting the polish on the last batch of 3 stories (18,500 words), and will send the first group of the Shaw letters. Not a line from them has ever been printed. No wonder! They are sassy and abuse America—a nice literary scandal is ahead. Last Friday, a week ago—Aug. 23rd, I sent the first batch of extracts from letters. I'm watching proof with unusual care—and, much cleaner proof it is than it was. What is this rumor that you, A. M., are to take the editorial and managerial reins of the N. Y. *Herald?* I only hope it's so. Count me as a critic on any old thing you say—if it is. Please don't forget to answer this letter—as you did my last. How about that syndicate proposition for "Avowals"?

As ever,

JIM.

Alden March.

To Frank J. Wilstach

1618 Beverly Road, Brooklyn
Sep. 9, 1918

DEAR FRANK:

Here are 2 new similes: "As prudent as an oyster." "As patient as a prostitute." From Phila. *Press* "Avowals of a Steeplejack"—J. G. H.

I finished 185,000 words in exactly 15 weeks— written with a pen, not dictated or typed. Series began June 9th—will run daily till Nov. 9th.

I'm used up and my annual hay fever is with me.

Hay-fever is hell. Tell me, Frank, at your leisure—
is Harry Nagle's last name spelled Neagle or Nagle?
I've written about the old *Recorder* days. But my
memory for proper names in treacherous. However, I shouldn't like Harry, himself, to know of this.
How are you? I'm printing some bully letters of
R. Mansfield in my story.

> With regards, as ever,
>
> Jim.

Frank Wilstach.

To Benjamin De Casseres

> The Royal Palace Hotel
> Atlantic City, N. J.
> Oct. 1st, 1918

Dear Ben:

But why do you address me at Phila.? I've never
left 1618 Beverly Road, Brooklyn, though I went
over two days weekly to write about music in Philadelphia for Mr. Wanamaker's newspaper. I'm down
here suffering from hay fever and will remain till
Oct. 17, when I return to N. Y. and begin on a morning newspaper—cobbling, half-soling, heeling and
blacking music-criticism. Alas! I've gone back to
the horrid abyss, Phlegethon. Simply had to. War
suppressed me as a writer. No wonder, La-bas! there
is something to write about. The Seven Arts go hang
in such a glorious time as this. Now—my nerves are

naked from writing—with a pen—185,000 words in 15 weeks (May 15-Aug. 29), for the Phila. *Press* appearing daily, week days only, since June 9. I enclose duplicate I had of 2nd day. It's a complete exposé of the mediocrity called J. G. H. from 1865 to 1915—50 years, Phila., Paris, N. Y. Hot stuff. Only last week I quoted you. Did your ears burn? In book form, I hope, next Spring, 1919. "Avowals of a Steeplejack" (though title may be changed). It's my property, not the *Press*—after Nov. 9. Saw the gracious reference in the *Sun* some weeks ago. Thanks! Am miserable with hay fever. Thirsty.

As ever,

JIM.

Ben De Casseres.

To H. L. Mencken

The Royal Palace Hotel
Atlantic City, N. J.
Oct. 13, 1918

DEAR HAL:

Magers sent me your characteristic and damned funny letter. Many a time my conscious twinged me, but just consider my awful season—2 or 3 times going over to Philadelphia, and writing Sunday stuff for the *Press;* and the still more awful 15 weeks last

Summer, when with a pen I wrote 185,000 words—
horrible for the *Press*. (Still going strong daily till
Nov. 9 like Johnny Walker.) So pity the laziness of
an old chap with a lost thirst. We return Oct. 21st.
I go with N. Y. *Times* this season. Music! Jessas,
Marie, Josef!

Gefülte fish with Med. Lots of Baltimore folk
here. Across street from George's uncle S. Nixon.
How are you! How is George! When we meet—
for pilsner must be on its way now—I'll tell you what
I think of music criticism. But Magers and March
certainly did make me happy in Phila. last season.
There's a chap here named Maurice Speiser who tells
me he has read with joy unconfined your article or
pamphlet on *Woman*. Won't you send me a copy
here. I'm dying to read it. Especially after what
Sen. Henry Cabot Lodge just wrote me about the de-
feat in the senate. I, too, paid my compliments to
Vance Thompson last week in the *Press* by simply
quoting what he wrote of the unfair sex in *Mlle.
New York* 25 years ago.

Have you read "A Story Teller's Holiday" by
George Moore? *The* limit. Amusing. Drop me a
line, Menck, and forgive my silence. I feel like a kid
out of jail with that writing job off my chest. Some
recollections!

As ever,

JIM.

H. L. Mencken.

To Richard Bach

Westminster Court
1618 Beverly Road
Brooklyn, N. Y.
Nov. 21, 1918

DEAR RICHARD:

Thanks for your letter with enclosed from Mr. Molaesky. When you write him thank him for me, tell him that I am sorry. I haven't an hour till next May. I'm glad to hear that Mrs. Beamish and the boy are in health again. It must have been a trying time last month for you all. I saw Maurice Speiser at the Prokokieff recital, and he told me that the *Evening Ledger* yesterday printed my story of the Phila. Orchestra with the head: "Special correspondent to the *E. L.*"—which I'm not. It's an old trick I hear—that is if it really appeared, and that I have no means of knowing as I haven't seen a copy of the paper in question. I write this, for, unimportant as it is, I should never become a correspondent to a Phila. paper without first asking permission of the *Press*. Voyous! Regards to you and yours and a handshake for the other "end of the sketch."

As ever,

JIM.

Richard Beamish.

To Mme. Frida Ashforth

Saturday A.M., Dec. 28, 1918

MY DEAR FRIDA:

The Patti picture in your letter gave me another pleasure. Thanks again. Patti was born 1843 (Barcelone), so that would make it 16 years old. Yes our Opera has no great singers, but it has a wonderful stage and orchestra. I'm sorry you didn't stay for "Gianni Schicchi" as it is the best music of the Puccini trio. "Oberon" is beautiful, and also "langweilig," the production magnificent. The new girl Rosa Ponselle has gold in her throat, but she has a lot to learn; and she lacks style! In Vaudeville a few months ago, all the more wonderful for that reason. I was shocked at Alice Mandelick's death. So young—after all. And the irony of fate, she is preached over by Percy Grant. Maupassant couldn't have wished a richer theme.

As ever,

JIM.

Mme. Frida Ashforth.

To Benjamin De Casseres

N. Y. *Times*
Sunday, Jan. 26, 1919

DEAR BEN:

Thank you for your continuing interest in "Steeple-jack." But not till Oct., 1919—if then—will it appear. As you may note I'm swamped in words and the Chicago Opera Co., opening tomorrow night. It is too much. I'll breathe freer in April—when the fast dwindling stock of beer shall have disappeared. O happy land of the free, home of the fanatic, America, I salute thee! I read you in the *Sun* or any other place you write, and always with interest. The prose-poem this morning was bully. You are individual.   With cordial sentiments,

As ever,

Ben De Casseres—poet!   JIM, the Penman.

To W. C. Brownell

1618 Beverly Road, Brooklyn
Feb. 19/19

DEAR MR. BROWNELL:

Thank you for the cheque from Messrs. Scribners, which is welcome. Nowadays a cheque is a benison. Oddly enough the "Iconoclasts" remains the "best seller" in my little collection of clotted nonsenses; and it is the worst I have thus far perpetrated! The hunger for propaganda in America is ferocious—

and grotesque. I really believe if I went in for the solemn mystic twaddle I might have more fame, more money (I have neither, as a matter of fact). Consider the cash of Elbert Hubbard! "Tu l'avez voulon" is right. I write: as they say in the sense of "on dit" or "man sagt," a colloquialism, and not literally. But it can be changed. By the way, I altered "A Book of Cities," subtitle, to "A Book of Images" as being not only more appropriate, but —it avoids repetition on the title page of the word "Cities" (an ugly word!). Certain European cities, etc. It also dodges the alliteration of Cosmopolis & Cities; while Images, its *m* echoes the *m* in Cosmopolis. How's that for verbalistic nonsense? I return, herewith, the page-proofs. The velocity with which this book has been read is sufficient comment on its absolute emptiness. Verb. sap! With thanks for your abiding interest,

I am sincerely,

JAMES HUNEKER.

To H. L. Mencken

1618 Beverly Road
Brooklyn, N. Y.
April 20/19

DEAR MENCK:

This is my first opportunity to tell you how touched (and also flattered, as I wrote John Williams), by the

gift so thoughtfully presented me at Sherry's by you
and George Jean. At once I carted it off to Mrs.
Morganatic, and since she writes the power-house is
completely swabbed out. All right, all right, for you
lads. I'll get uneven later. I'll send you "Amber-
gris" next week. I'm up against 4,000 words for
Smith (Slush, drool, drivel, about the musical season and garden sprinklers, etc.!) Hope to see you
oftener now that the thaw has set in.

Cordially,

JIM.

H. L. Mencken.

To T. R. Smith

1618 Beverly Road
Brooklyn, N. Y.
April 22, 1919

DEAR SMITH, T. R.:

Enclosed the story—over 4,000 words, nearer 5
than 4. It was completed yesterday one day later
than promised, to my disgust, for I work by schedule,
and usually keep my word. But—on my back since
Saturday suffering, bladder, spasms in urethra, painful micturition—you know the list of symptoms, etc.,
etc. Too much uric, nothing else. I lay low this
week. No morganatic calisthenics! The story is
written in the newspaper, not the "Stately" Magazine

style; *i.e.*, colloquial and straight from the shoulder. I've told some unpalatable truths. No libels—no *double-entendres*. Facts! I hope you like it. Considering my continual pain during the writing the handwriting is comparatively clear. Tell your proof-readers that I underscore u̱; and overscore n—thus, It saves trouble. I should like to see galley-proof soon. So many proper names. I'll return in 24 hours corrected. I've written Mr. Liveright in this mail. Friday is not possible for luncheon. I'm ill, irritable and dieting. Next week! The scheme, in reality your scheme, sounds good to me. As to the "Steeplejack," the book is in the hands of another publisher—long since promised. On its return you shall see it, of course.

With apologies for delayed music story.

I am, as ever,

JAMES HUNEKER.

T. R. Smith.

P. S.—Perhaps the view of that amorous warming-pan which Mencken and George Jean presented me last week may have caused the derangement in my uro-genital system. (As the late Diamond Jim Brady would call it if he were still p——g on our planet.)

To T. R. Smith

1618 Beverly Road
Brooklyn, N. Y.
May 1, 1919

DEAR T. R.:

I return cheque. You told me $250 at Sherry's. You also wrote me those figures. You will find that the story is at least 4,000 words. Also that I have covered the field—a few words omitted which I had intended putting in when the galleys came. If you had some distinct policy why didn't you say so? I didn't deal largely with the Chicago Co., because, with the exception of Garden & Baklanoff, the organization isn't worth powder and shot to blow it to hell. I think I've landed a few punches. But send the story back, old man. I can sell it for $300 within 48 hours, if it doesn't suit. I don't like an editor to take anything unsatisfactory. Remember, too, it had to be a swift bird's-eye view, hence superficial. Ship it back! I was operated on last night for a cyst in my bladder. I've been suffering torture for the past 10 days; and today I'm no better. What the hell! I can only die once—and diabetes is such a sweet death!

Cordially,

JAMES HUNEKER.

T. R. Smith.

To Burton Rascoe

1618 Beverly Road
Brooklyn, N. Y.
May 8/19

DEAR MR. RASCOE:

I am on a bed of pain; inflammation (serves me jolly well right for being an anti-prohibitionist) so do, pray, pardon this tardy, brief reply to your letters and articles. What a splendid young pen, bald to audacity, and brilliant, you possess! Your page* is a corker, and with Elia Peattie it is hard to beat; not East is it beaten. You surmised correctly—there

*The page he refers to was the literary page conducted for two years in the Chicago *Tribune*. . . . I had been puzzled by the fact that the two greatest literary men of their time—Anatole France and Remy de Gourmont—had never taken any notice of each other, although both of them had written vast numbers of critical notices and reviews. France reviewed Gourmont's *Le Latin Mystique* but nowhere else mentions him; and Gourmont refers to France only casually three or four times in the whole body of his critical work. I asked Mr. Huneker for his explanation of this indifference to each other, suggesting that possibly it had its origin in that famous preface to the second series of *La Vie Litteraire*, wherein France poked fun at Gourmont's particular admiration, the Symbolists, and made out elaborately that they were diseased and proud of their disease. The situation probably really arose out of France's review of *Le Latin Mystique*; both men were scholars in and had a profound love for medieval literature,

was a distinct coolness between St. Anatole and St. Remy—what it precisely was Remy would not tell me: I had noted the hiatus; possibly both men were "working the same side of the street"—called Ironic Skepticism! I fancy the diseased poets had little to do with the matter. Way off in the early eighties the thing began. Dear Remy! It was like a voice from the grave to read that paragraph. I, too, am hoping to see you in the flesh, and thank you for your courtesy. Sincerely,

JAMES HUNEKER.

Burton Rascoe.

To Alden March

1618 Beverly Road
Brooklyn, N. Y.
May 12/19

DEAR ALDEN:

Thanks for the pictures.* Phew! what a crossgrained, cantankerous old b—d I am. Now, I'm on

particularly decadent Latin and ecclesiastical Latin. France's review might easily have been construed as patronizing and rather too much "talking of himself apropos" of Remy de Gourmont. And Gourmont, too, had his vanity. The paragraph was one I marked in a translation if made of a paper by Gourmont on French books in America.

BURTON RASCOE.

* Of himself.

a milk diet—forever (inflammation bladder, operation, etc.), and my expression is perfectly angelic. I'll return to mast—— next—idyll of our boyhood days!

Cordially,

JIM.

Alden March.

To W. B. Chase

Westminster Court
Brooklyn, N. Y.
Monday, May 12, 1919

DEAR BILL:

The article—which reads as if written by a perfectly deodorized female—should have been headed "Art and Alcohol" ("Denatured"). However, it's all in the day's work.

Thanks for Billy *G's* clipping. But he is wrong. My father was *not* a Hungarian, nor his father, grandfather; perhaps his great-grandfather was prior to 1750, the date in the town chronicles when the first Huneker settled in Phila. So much for Billy's ingenuous attempt to join me to the "Jewish race!" Enclosed please set up and mail proof down here, as I really can't say whether I'll be over Tuesday, Wednesday, or Friday. It depends on the health of my old girl. Leave my letters where I can get them; either in my drawer or in your desk exposed. You

will find naught to "edit" in this story. It's plain
and damned unvarnished sailing.

Thank you, Bill.

As ever,

JIM.

W. B. Chase.

P. S.—I fancy the Sunday stuff will stop (by
command) after the last Sunday, May 25th. That's
the way I feel now, though I can turn out "copy" all
summer if asked.

To T. R. Smith

1618 Beverly Road
Brooklyn, N. Y.
May 20, 1919

DEAR T. R.:

How you do flatter me! Apart altogether from a
sadly leaking p . . . . . . o I can't leave the Missus—
who is still helpless, though not hopeless—in bed.
I've been out, but buttermilk and banana legs are
not firmly planted legs; enfin. I'm still weak, and
while that projected party "sounds good to me," I
can't join thirsts with the gang. Remember me! And
thanks.

As ever,

JIM.

T. R. Smith.

To Richard Bach

1618 Beverly Road
Brooklyn, N. Y.
May 26, 1919

DEAR RICHARD BACH:

Almost thou persuadest me to become a—Philadelphian. Isn't it the damnest thing the way subtle appeals are dangled? I suppose an appeal can "dangle"; mine did when I was young and lusty— before my eyes. 1st, there's the *Press* with Alden and you and Magers; 2nd, there's Phila. itself with its invitation, to comfortable, reasonable, *human* living; 3rd, and now the Craven house—a gem of a place, either furnished or unfurnished. What to do? I've the *Times* for another season if I wish it—but *not* music or drama. I was half killed last season; although hard work never killed a Huneker. Just get close to Jim Craven, will you, Richard, and without asking him precise figures, let him give you an idea —I suppose something fierce! And then drop me the hint, here.

In a night I became a teetotaller, though I still loathe prohibition. I live on bananas and buttermilk. I am well. (Knock wood.) I haven't missed beer or ale or wine. I'll never drink again, for, manifestly, if you can stop 4 weeks as I have done, you can stop forever (but—Damn the Kaiser! He is to blame for rotten beer here, and still rottener pro-

hibition). But, my God! You should see me eat!
Phew—3 meals a day and furtive rummaging in
midnight pantries for pie. So here I am a young
fellow nearly 3 score, healthy—happy that my be-
loved rib is getting better—but not yet wise. Do
drop me a line. Love to Alden and regards to Mrs.
Beamish.

As ever,

JIM.

Richard Beamish.

To W. C. Brownell

Westminster Court
1618 Beverly Road
Brooklyn, N. Y.
June 15/19

MY DEAR MR. BROWNELL:

Of course, you are right, and if you had presented
1,000 more reasons against the inclusion of those
letters, I couldn't say nay! But one thing is overlooked, the vital issue which reduces to the futile,
to the academic discussion of the matter; *i.e.*, will or
will not the letters sell the book? All other consid-
erations are naught to me. The London sales would
be negligible—they always have been with my books;
but the American sales might not be. Even a success de scandale! Anything but the collecting of
dust on top-shelves! I am through with such non-

sense; as, for example, non-ethical, lack of taste,
etc. The two offending words, sodomy and flagella-
mania, do occur in a quasi-scientific communication,
and to speak of their exclusion makes me rub my
eyes. Is this 1880 or 1920? (besides the flagellation
allusion of Shaw refers to the public flogging of sailors and soldiers, in the British navy and army, a
cruel custom which he helped to stop with the aid
of certain distinguished humanitarians; as to the sodomy—well, he doesn't indict the entire nation; all
nations have that particular black beast in "their
midst," and the Wilde scandal with its horrid publicity has inured the public to the word, which by the
way, is not employed offensively). However, these
are minor splotches. The chief thing is—will Shaw
consent? You think the tale of our quarrel stale and
silly. Soit? But the book is composed of ancient
and often silly memories. That's why I wrote it—
en souvenir. I believe the letters will materially swell
the sales here or in London. You do not. A difference of opinion, but a serious one to our bank ac-
counts. Sodomy, what will you say to the "Mary
Garden" book, with its milanga of essays (?) and
short stories, many of them morbid, even risky. As
to my novel—now well under way—it will shock
you, I'm sure, as the title-page bears this motto from
Walt Whitman's poem (?) "A Woman Waits for
Me," "All were lacking if the moisture of the right
man were lacking." In a word, the book is frankly

erotic—though well within the law. I hardly think your house would print it. When Mr. Scribner wired me, and later wrote, I was told that what I chose to print would be tolerated by him. Already you are balking. It was for this precise reason that I had considered the offers of another publisher, one who wanted the book because of the Shaw letters. He was willing to take the risks of lawsuits, etc. You are not. Now why shouldn't I write G. B. S.? If he says no, then you will know how to act. I haven't given up hope yet. But one thing I insist on, even if it comes to a disagreement—my copy must go in as it appeared in the *Press*. All of it—not only the Shaw letters. I must not be hampered by any moral, so-called reasons. I'm weary of the dusty primrose path and—well, my dear W. C., this is 1920, isn't it? We are in for a puritanical suppression of individuality at all costs, so I'm taking time by the forelock (not foreskin, as you may think)! As a matter of fact, there is nothing in "Steeplejack" or "Mary Garden" (the book, not the adorable girl) that is vulgar, obscene, or, I hope, tasteless—except those damnable Shaw letters, and they are so brimful of vitality, and sparkling apercus, that I honestly believe that I should be a public benefactor, if, aided and abetted by Charles Scribner's Sons, I gave them to the world. (Of course, this is only self-mystification, but I enjoy it.) If G. B. S. consents then the letters must be printed. Do you consent? Rather, do you advise me to ask him—and, oh! what a row will be precipitated. I'm sorry to bother you with all this trivial talk, but let us get through with it as soon as possible.

Sincerely, as ever,

JAMES HUNEKER.

W. C. Brownell.

To Maxwell E. Perkins

Westminster Court
June 25/19

DEAR MR. PERKINS:

A woman rang me up yesterday. She belongs to a little so-called Art magazine. She told my wife—as I was not at home—that Mr. Scribner had consented to the republication of one of my articles from my "Promenades." Furthermore, she was so blithely impertinent as to say that I should call her up this morning, otherwise the article in question would be reprinted, as they were "pressed for time"! I don't know whether you know who gave this alleged permission without first consulting me, but do please make inquiries, and tell whoever it may be, not to give assent to any such swindling propositions. They are trying to get something for nothing, and to that game I vigorously object, all the more so, as last season they reprinted an article of mine on Frank Brangwin, the Etcher, from "Promenades," and ab-

solutely without my consent or even knowledge till
months afterwards. If they would pay a sum—say
$100—then it would be different. Mr. Brownell
suggests that in that case a fair division would be
made with Scribners; but this god-damned "nervy"
way of 'phoning and informing you that etc., etc.,
Jesus! It's absurd to get hotter on a hot day over
such a little matter, but when Rodin died I had to
call down the *Evening Post* (sanctified) for printing a lengthy—about a page—of my Rodin study in
the "Promenades"; and shortly afterwards the *Tribune* for using without the ghost of an acknowledgment, my Flaubert letter from "Egoists." Sorry to
bother you. Life is so short and sweaty. Thanks
for Galsworthy book, which is due! I'll write a
blurb for "Steeplejack" next Sunday.

Cordially,

JAMES HUNEKER.

Maxwell E. Perkins.

To Maxwell E. Perkins

Westminster Court
June 28/1919

DEAR MR. PERKINS:
  Here is the blurb for "Steeplejack" Jacket. A
rotten job. If I don't set forth the "incomparable"
merits of this "unique" book, then the blurb no longer
blurbs; if I told the brutal truth you wouldn't print

it. And if I say nice sweet phrases then—that way egotism lies. So I did what most people do when they must face the music of facts: I dodged, I hope I may see a proof, or, at least a clean typescript? Thanks for your letter this morning which came in company with a hot morsel of abuse from an outraged petticoat pan. I dared to ask that we be paid for the privilege of reproduction! I was *afraid* enough to tell that the (magazine) editors were trying to get something for nothing; *hinc illæ*, etc. Your letter was a submission—breeding club, as the lady had deliberately—well, let us say—exaggerated. All's well that ends in a riddance to such bad rubbish.

Sincerely,
JAMES HUNEKER.

Maxwell E. Perkins.

To John Quinn

1618 Beverly Road
Brooklyn, N. Y.
July 15, 1919

MY DEAR JOHN:

First, let me apologize for not answering your letter. 2nd, let me thank you *in re* Lady Gregory. It was kind of you to bother yourself asking her and kind of her to so graciously assent. If you write her

I wish you would thank her for me. I'm glad you are away, and, I hope, resting; that is, if your busy skull can take a holiday. I'll wager you are at the long distance with Curtin at the N. Y. end, and all day at that.

What about Irish Valera and his scheme; pleasing proposition. But I'd like to hear Horace Plunkett's opinion of Carson—his private opinion.

You are quite right in guessing syphilis in the case of B——. His hair dropped off—hence the green soap and the green-haired legend. Add—Poe, Nietzsche, Maupassant, Manet—a sad case indeed,

Pallida Spirochæta—the parasite of syphilis, not the germ itself—spares no one. You missed a hell of a hot spell, July 2nd to 5th or 6th.

Another is due. (I've written to G. B. S.) We are, neither of us, lively. I have no "urge," as Walt W. says. No booze since April 27th, and never miss it; yet I believe alcohol is a driving force when taken moderately. The *Times* has asked me to go to Europe.

I've signed a fresh lease down here. The rental increase is not to be prohibitive. I can't get away till 1920. I'm writing 10,000 words weekly (also weakly and methodically), for my new autumn book, 1920, with a pen. It's to be 100,000 words. Fiction. "Steeplejack" (Oct., 1919) 2 big volumes is defecating proof. I'm busy. Then the weekly stunt in the *Times*.

We must eat, even if we can't drink. And the Mary Garden book for Jan. 15, 1920.

Yes, on the whole, I'm a trifle occupied. Now John, pardon my loose correspondence. Get strong and return in fighting trim. You are naturally belligerent.

With love from Jozio and
JAMES.

John Quinn.

To Mme. Frida Ashforth

1618 Beverly Road
Brooklyn, N. Y.
Aug. 1st/19

MY DEAR FRIDA:

By this time you know that singers are always ungrateful. Ingratitude is the badge of their tribe, so the young person's behaviour is not at all enigmatic. Depend upon it she won't cut much—operatic. "Elle est une arrivista." She can't keep in the picture like Fritzi Scheff, whose logical place was in operetta. Therefore, my dear girl, why waste good emotions on such a thankless little egotist. You surprise me, and at your mature age allowing a cub that isn't housebroken to agitate your heartstring. Cheer up! Aldrich is coming back to his old job on the *Times,* and I shall have to abdicate. If you would know the reason why I'm glad, just read the

Century magazine for July. "The High Lights of the Musical Season."

We are glad to know you are well. We are pegging along. I am having laborious days. I am, in addition to writing my Sunday *Times* article, reading proof of my new book—or books, two big volumes —which comes out in October. *"Steeplejack,"* is the title, and it is a book of recollections dating from Lincoln's funeral in 1865—my earliest memory— to 1917, when we went into war to free the world from autocracies (nicht!) *You* may recall that I told you about the work—it *is* a *work*—last Summer when I wrote 185,000 words in 15 weeks for the Philadelphia *Press,* in whose columns these souvenirs ran daily for 5 months. Now it's in book form. I'll send you a copy when it appears. (But proofreading is the least of my present tasks, I'm chained to my ink well—*Your* old present—writing 10,000 words weekly for my new book to appear Oct., 1920. It's fiction. My first novel began. *You* are in it, your name undisguised; but don't worry, Frida. I've not put you in any trying positions. I must write in all 100,000 words. I've finished 40,000 words. I still have 60,000 ahead of me; two awful months. This is my vacation. And no beer, no wine. (Fornication is forgotten—and thank the Lord.) Good age, dear Frida!

Love from Josie and

JIM.

To Benjamin De Casseres

1618 Beverly Road
Brooklyn, N. Y.
Sep. 27, 1919

DEAR BEN:

Enclosed should really be in your hands. It should also prove pleasant reading. I had hoped to run across you sometime, somewhere, somewhen and deliver the message vive voce, but as I go away next week for a month, A. C.-N. J., same old hotel Royal Palace "on the boardwalk"—I send the message. But don't tell E. S. you have it.

I'm worn out reading proof of "Steeplejack"; reading 2 sets of proof, and in 1918 I had, not only to write the stuff, but to read galley-proof for the Phila. *Press*. Naturally I loathe the book which is due next month, about the middle.

Ill as I was from bladder trouble—5 months on water wagon now—I composed and wrote a novel— 100,000 words. A naked horror it is. I wrote it in 7 weeks, less 2 days—wrote with the tears in my eyes from age; and in revenge I hope there will not be a dry seat (female) after reading it. Of course I planned the "machine" for months; the writing of it was but the final ejaculation of the verbal sperm. But I wrote it with a pen—207 of my yellow sheets; wrote 10 or 12 thousand words a week, even more. Never again. It's slated for Oct., 1920, *i.e.*, if the police, prompted by the society for the prevention of cruelty to imbeciles, don't intervene.

Tomorrow, Sep. 28, my last script appears in N. Y. *Times*. Aldrich returns. I don't like editorial work —sand and linoleum—so I'll write "specials" for Sundays in October, beginning Oct. 5, N. Y. *World*. (Keep this dark till then.) I may go to Europe in November—I hope not. 3 per cent beer in Germany, and anarchy everywhere. I'm too old.

Happy New Year. Gut Jontov!

Cordially, as ever,

JIM, the Penman.

Ben De Casseres.

To H. L. Mencken

1618 Beverly Road
Brooklyn, N. Y.
Nov. 5/19

DEAR HAL:

Just returned from a week at that epitome of charmlessness, Atlantic City. Hence, I didn't acknowledge either to you or Knopf the book. And now at the risk of evoking from you a cynical quotation from Doctor Johnson ("the reciprocal civilities of authors," etc.) I'm going to report what I told Knopf: *i.e.*, that "Prejudices" is your biggest most brilliant volume of criticism. You have us *all* lashed to the mast. You are *It* in the American criti-

cal circus. All the rest are fading ghosts. You have
smashed records in hitting bullseyes. Having carefully shaved the victim let me settle down to shop.
Printers have played hob with "Steeplejack." My
"Mary Garden" is due Feb., 1920, but——! The
novel, after 2 months in Miss Oehler's hands, is arrived today. I read half in Atlantic City, and am
busy correcting the rest now. She says she typed the
stuff wearing a gas mask, but after reading a lot of
the new English Johnnies, I find my story rather pal-
lid; but, Menck, it is at least a story. Miss O., a com-
petent judge from the "peepul," told me she was all
"het" up over the story *per se* (without the omphalic
trimmings).

I'll have it licked into shape in a week or two.
You said you would read it. It's about 75,000 words.
I fear cuts because the two breaks, rather digressions,
are to give air, a *lunga pausa* in the current of a
helter-skelter swift narrative. Besides serving as the
inescapable throw-back, or retrospective, they further
serve as an exposition of my hero's (a sorry one)
character, tastes, aptitudes. I started to write a psychological study of character. I didn't succeed.
There are enough happenings to amuse the choicest
company at a bordel. Therefore, ergo—couldn't I
sell the novel, serial rights, to *S. S.* as it stands, and
have you print it in, say, 3 numbers. Price, if you
like the stuff, to be discussed.

My hour of travail is at hand. I begin daily work

this evening. I love it—nicht. It's a hard winter ahead for newspaper men, hence my desire to sell something.

Let me hear from you at your leisure. How did you like "Avowals"? I haven't seen S. S. this month.

Regards to G. J. N. and to yourself. (The wets may win out yet!)

                    As ever,
H. L. Mencken.   JIM.

To T. R. Smith

                    1618 Beverly Road
                    Brooklyn, N. Y.
                    Nov. 28/19

MY DEAR TOM:

You will certainly see the story when S. & S. get through with it next week; then I must bring it home for a few days to cobble up the carbon copy—it is uncorrected, and there are lacunæ and it is the only copy in case the original got lost. So—week after next and I'll fetch it in myself. But really there is no hurry. You are filled with the Louys and new Moore volumes; mine will keep a few weeks. As to the bowdlerization nothing is decided upon. The story can stand on its merits without the humorous elements; of obscenity, vulgarity or indecency, there is not a trace; only extreme frankness and the sex side dealt with as if by a medical expert. Might I say—gynecologist? You are very kind to take such interest. To you shall go the next reading.

As ever,

T. R. Smith.   JIM.

To T. R. Smith

1618 Beverly Road
Brooklyn, N. Y.
Dec. 7, 1919

DEAR TOM:

I fetched the story home from Scribner's yesterday, and today and tomorrow, I am working on the carbon copy, making corrections and interlineations— in one case a page long. Thursday next, Dec. 11th, I shall call at your office between 12 and 1 o'clock to hand the original typescript to you. Let me know if you will be there; or with whom I shall leave the damnable stuff. I should like very much to see you for 15 minutes. I have the N. Y. Symphony at Carnegie Hall at 3 p. m., so time is limited; another concert in the evening same place, and between the two, I earn my living—as the little girl said of her legs; *i.e.,* I write my criticism at office, bolt my dinner and rush into the Philharmonic fray at 8.30. A hell of a life for a lazy man, as I am. Drop me a line here, never at *World*. Letters there go astray—

frequently. Hope you are well and thirsty. I am—
Toujours! As ever,

JIM.

T. R. Smith.

To John Quinn

Westminster Court
1618 Beverly Road
Brooklyn, N. Y.
Dec. 30/19

MY DEAR JOHN:

The top of the New Year to ye, my lad! I shan't
apologize for my silence; my work has cruelly pressed
me, as you may know. I'm working double-tides on
the *World;* art and music. It's not easy. Enclosed
may appall you. Just read at haphazard and return
at leisure. My novel will very likely appear in the
same season as George Moore's "Storyteller's Holiday," "Avowals," &c. The next to appear is "Aphro-
dite," then "Istar"—title not yet decided on; either
"Istar" (daughter of sin, you recall the old Baby-
lonial epic) or "Painted Veils." But the chief point
is that the story thus far has laid the experts out
cold. Scribners, who want the book to publish *expurgated,* told me—and I blush to repeat the words!
—that not in this generation have they read a fiction
so original, brilliant, *human,* or so well composed
and written! The joke is, John, that I wrote the
damned thing in 7 *weeks,* less 2 days, although I

planned it for 2 months. What pleases me most—
and all this must seem naïve to you, but it's my first
full sized fiction (at 60!) therefore, my darling Benjamin among my books—is, that Mencken is pleased.
In "Prefaces" dealing with my work, he said I had
no particular aptitude for fiction—and the many in-
ventions, fantastic, exotic, extravagant though they
be, of "Melomaniacs" and "Visionaries" staring him
in the face. But he errs in believing "Istar" is only
a novel of lascivious frills and thrills. I wrote it
because I had a story to tell, because it is largely
characterization, with plenty of action. It may be
made into a play next summer. Now—if you should
care to read it in clean, clear typescript, I'll fetch you
a copy. The chief thing is that I should like you to
see the publisher's contract. I need money and I'm
going to get it. First the unexpurgated copy; then,
later, for the purer public, the bowdlerized edition—
catch them going and coming!

As ever,

John Quinn.   JIM.

To T. R. Smith

1618 Beverly Road
Brooklyn, N. Y.
Dec. 30, 1919

DEAR TOM:

I'm reading galleys of the Mary Garden book,
due Feb. 15. And that reminds me you haven't

written concerning Istar. Have you read it? Has Horace B. read it? The reason I ask is not because other publishers are clamoring for a peep in at it, but because S. & S. would like to publish it this Spring expurgated. But I think it could be handled so that it might be printed first unexpurgated—later for the purer public. I am having a slight surcease of work this week after the Blue (Bird) T——d rot; which isn't worth the critical powder and shot to blow it hellwards; either music, or book, or production. I'm therefore free for at least one day this week, next Saturday, Jan. 3rd. Will there be any chance of seeing you then, say at one p. m.? If not I'll have to dig up another date for next week—which will not be easy. Let me hear from you in either case. And will you be so kind as to send me an editorial copy of your Baudelaire edition? I'm really interested to see what you did with it. If Brentanos hadn't asked me long before you did to furnish that introduction, I should have been glad to give it to your publication. Happy New Year. And now that repetitions have begun at the Opera, I'll fix you with a couple of seats when it is possible—you to pick your night.

As ever,

JIM.

T. R. Smith.

< 1920 >

To T. R. Smith

1618 Beverly Road
Brooklyn, N. Y.
Jan. 1, 1920

DEAR TOM:

Happy New Year to you and yours! (This in-
cludes morganatic and otherwise.) To my surprise
—and horror—I have just learned that I am not free
next Saturday, although I chucked 2 piano recitals
to be with you. The Missus—She Who Must Be
Obeyed! as Rider Haggard puts it—made an im-
perative engagement for me, behind my back, without my knowledge or consent! A sort of rape en
famille! So let's put off that meeting till sometime
next week, any midday except Monday and Tuesday.
I'm sorry. I've dropped a line to H. L. thanking
him in advance for the gifts. Legal and literary
advice prompt me to tell you that Istar expurgated
may also enjoy a success—presuming, of course, that
she will be successful unexpurgated. Nous verrons.

Sincerely, as ever,

T. R. Smith.   JIM.

To Maxwell E. Perkins

Flatbush, Monday, Jan. 5/20

MY DEAR MR. PERKINS:

I find I can't get in to see you this afternoon as
promised, and I'll try tomorrow or Thursday. But I

enclose title-page, the blurb for the Jacket, also the acknowledgment to various magazines and newspapers from which the papers are taken. I believe it is now a matter for copyright purposes. The blurb is as carefully constructed as I could make it; it embodies, I think, the chief idea on which we agreed— *i.e.*, that M. G. was to be pictured—en vignetta, or anyhow—that her name appears in bold lettering; that the general tenor of the book's contents be dwelt upon. These things I have done. I thought a reference to the fiction would not come amiss, since diabolism, mysticism, and other engaging superstitions are rife just now in the land; therefore, I lugged in the names of Tolstoy & Huysmans in regard to the last Devil, Worship Tale, "The Vision Malefic." As regards Mary and her little lamb of a temperament, I may only quote the brief remark of one of the best-known book salesmen in New York. "Her name on the cover of a book is the best of commercial propositions!" And this is the consensus of "professional" opinions on the only act. The same was practically said at Brentano's. You know the man from whom I quote. I mention all this dear Perkins, merely to show you that I spoke by the card when I insisted on the inclusion of her name, if not on the title-page then on the Jacket. I hope you will back me up in this for I've made the concession demanded by Mr. W. C. B. and now it's your turn to play fair. Last May I was promised two

things; one was "Steeplejack," and the strike killed
that chance. Now my original scheme of entitling the
book with her name is upset. I'm through, I assure
you. I'll not make any more suggestions, but if
this Jacket idea is killed then I object to any title
except the original. As to the pictures—they can be
soon arranged. I take no more interest in "Steeplejack," which will be stale when published, and little
if any in the Garden book, unless you comply with
my not too exigent request.

Sincerely,

JAMES HUNEKER.

Maxwell E. Perkins.

To John Quinn

Jan. 6, 1920

MY DEAR JOHN:

You are certainly a brick to read at a gallop that
story of mine. I'm delighted that you find it good
in spots. The other critical chaps are excellent
courts of appeal; but for me you are the supreme
court of criticism. The chief objection to the book
is that it is not beautiful; that it may be amusing,
but that it leaves the emotions untouched. That, and
the absence of cadenced prose, are the penalties paid
for racing with my pen in seven weeks what should
have been seventy months. However, it's only a
starter, a little canter for a speed trial: besides, it is

really a play, conceived as a play, has the scenario effect of a play, falls into the divisions of a play, with its scene a faire: the knocking at the door and howling for a sperma injection, is dramatic, nay theatric: hence you felt its artificiality: and it is that. I fear Ulick can't be changed. It's a common enough name. Of course "naked wars" is to go in quotes. I'm surprised about missing pages. The copy in the hand of Smith is perfect. I'll get after the typist: she may have overlooked them. The "missing theme—or musical motion" is not alone the stripping of Istar, but is the discovery that she was raped by Brother Rainbow in the early chapters, and it was only revealed in the last pages to Ulick. That item I kept as close to the symphonic poem "Istar" by Vincent D'Indy—a charming work: otherwise I played freely with the scheme, which was, as I told you, only a sort of restraining fervor for my loose impressionism and tendency to improvise. My next novel—a larger canvas—will not be so speedy, and I hope not so staccato. The rhythms in "Istar" are too choppy: you miss the long rhythmic roll of both Conrad and Moore. But, then, they are great artists. I am only a newspaper man. At any rate you don't know a picture just like it, do you? It's more French in style and construction than English. And that is what I was after. The story itself is largely true. I know—and knew—Istar. She is a composite of— well, I'll tell you some day. Mona is in town today:

and the little slut, Dora, still lives and ceased fornication. She is rich. She cries when we meet.
Sentiment tempered by rum. The Pie girl dinner
occurred at a studio. Saint-Gaudens modelled a mon-
ster phallis. I had the photo of it. Some of the
girls were famous as models and chorus girls.
Ulick is we all. Milt is a bore, but I like Albert
Stone—he is dead, but he lived. The scheme is a
6 part—or voiced—fugue in which the themes wind
in and out. It is musical or nothing, John!

John Quinn.
                    Thanks again,
                                        JIM.

To T. R. Smith

Thursday, Feb. 5, 1920

DEAR TOM:

I couldn't get in to see you Wednesday, as I said I
would. But I'll be in next Saturday morning before
noon. Leave the mss. with your people for me. You
couldn't wrap up in the bundle that copy of John
Cleland's masterpiece. I'll be careful of it, and it
won't leave my hands. I'll be glad if you can do
this.

Regarding Monday at the opera, I must "cover" it
myself for not only does Matzenauer sing Amneris
this season, but Clarence Whitehill returns to the
Metropolitan.

However, there are other operas from which you

may take your pick, except Thursday, when I must again "cover" the return of Barrientos. Carmen— Wednesday evening, Farrar-Martinelli. La Bohème, Friday evening. The Matinee my wife goes—always. Let me know by Monday morning in case I don't see you Saturday, and I'll mail the seats at once. There are weeks ahead yet, Tom, when the repetitions begin. Don't forget Fanny—I haven't read the baggage for 30 years.

As ever,

T. R. Smith.   JIM.

To Dr. T. C. Williams

1618 Beverly Road
Brooklyn, N. Y.
Feb. 26, 1920

MY DEAR TOM:

Next Friday, March 5th, Caruso and Matzenauer, and Musio sing "The Prophet" at the Metropolitan Opera House. Artur Bodanzsky conducts. It is one of the most stunning productions of the season. Wouldn't you like to go and take your best girl— Miss Fallopian Tubes? Say the word—*not* over the phone as we are seldom home—in a note and I'll send you 2 seats.

P. S.   *Entre nous*, strictly—put all visits and medical attendance of Rhoda on my bill. I don't want her to pay, and I don't want you to be troubled by

patients who can't pay.   So please do me the favor
and keep it to yourself.   *She* has done us a 1,000
favors, is still doing them.   She has a heart of gold.

As ever,

"slightly pregnant" with ideas,

Cordially,

JAMES.

Dr. Thomas C. Williams.

To John Quinn

> 1618 Beverly Road
> Brooklyn, N. Y.
> March 7, 1920

MY DEAR JOHN:

It is your letter that is a corker, not "Bedouins"
(a confusing book at best).   "Jurgen" I read and
marvelled over—at the notion of it being obscene.
It is, as a literary performance, a clever pasticcio;
the shell not the interior glow of both Rabelais and
Anatole France.   But cold, as cold as they are spontaneous.   As for the immorality, Smith of the *Century* is right when he said to me that if there is
obscenity or immorality in the book it is Fourth-
Dimensional immorality.   Not bad.   Since Smith
wrote a claimant letter from Horace Liveright.   Now
he wants to reconsider.   Much depends on the Jurgen decision.   Both he and Knopf got cold feet.

But, would you? Don't you think that I had better make about twenty excisions and let the book appear for the sake of the story? I re-read it and edited about six hundred words from it, and I believe to the advantage of the tale. If it can't stand alone for its characterization and narrative, then it is worthless. The lascivious frills are only frills. I think I'll risk it—other publishers than S. & S.—but I should very much like to have your personal opinion —at your leisure, of course. The *Tribune* has given "Bedouins" a big send off this morning, not critical, but as a newspaper display. I wish to get out "Istar" in two months. It is summer fiction and perhaps it might sell. As to Saturday next: unfortunately I have the Josef Hoffman last recital of the season at Carnegie. We must meet, and let it be my first free Saturday, as I don't want to run away. Frank Cobb often speaks of you. In the same mail as your letter was one from George Wickersham. He never forgets our early days. Law and order represented by George and the *dis* by myself. I'll write to you as soon as I see the concert schedule, but it won't be the 20th inst., as that is the last Boston Symphony matinee. Perhaps March 27, but I'll let you know. Love from house to house.

As ever,

JAMES.

John Quinn.

To T. R. Smith

1618 Beverly Road
Brooklyn, N. Y.
March 9, 1920

DEAR TOM:

Always the week before—then I can supply you. Every ticket was given out last Saturday. I'm sorry. But next week's announcements are due tomorrow and just pick your night—any one that is not a novelty—*i.e.*, first night; or next Monday night, which is reserved. I'll be in next week some midday fetching Fanny's first play. It has not left my possession for 5 minutes; it will be intact, plates, etc., even if Fornicating Fanny was not "virgo intacta"; furthermore, I didn't show it to any one—not even my Missus. (Sinister laughter!) Why should you? asks the devil's advocate. John Quinn is to represent McBride. He may get "Jurgen" across—it's as dangerous as a caterpillar.   "A Bientot,"

As ever,

T. R. Smith.   JIM.

1618 Beverly Road
Brooklyn, N. Y.
March 10, 1920

DEAR TOM:

Thank you for the very handsome book, which arrived a few hours after I wrote you yesterday. The pictures are excellent. Let's go to the South seas and change our luck! Also *pour attraper quelque-chose*—for they say Syph. rages mightily on those islands.

The opera list for next week is out, I can offer you Wed. "L'Elisir d'Amora" with Caruso, Scotti, &c., or Friday, "Parsifal" (wow!). "Zaza" is pre-scripted, and "Manon," and my Missus takes the Sat. matinee. So let me know by Monday.

Cordially,

JIM.

T. R. Smith.

To T. R. Smith

1618 Beverly Road
Brooklyn, N. Y.
March 14, 1920

DEAR TOM:

Here are the seats. I hope you can use them. May I impose on your good nature again? I should very much like to keep "Fanny" till Monday, March 22nd—eight days from tomorrow. May I? It is a very important seduction, I assure you—not a virgin ("Maidenheads are for plowboys," roars Doc Johnson), but something far finer, far more spiritual. A conversion! Nothing more nor less than the conversion of a Lesbian lady to the strait and narrow patch of normal fornication. "Fanny" and the charming vignettes will compass my idealistic end. Explain this to the owner of the book; say that a work of virtue is to be accomplished. St. Priapus of the Holy Church of Heavenly Nesting may answer my prayers. I vow to bring in the treasure next week—after the 22nd. If it is too much to ask, let me know and I'll be in this week.

Cordially,

JIM, the Penman.

T. R. Smith.

To Dr. T. C. Williams

Flatbush: Adjacent to all Cemeteries,
Mar. 17, 1920

DEAR DOCTOR:

I left a gold necktie clasp on mantelpiece in your maternity ward last night (or, should I say paternity?). Please save it for me till I go in next week. Water broke last night. Dry or breech presentation I fear. But while there's a Krysteller plug there's hopes for a woman!

JIM, the Penman

[Postal to]
Dr. Thomas C. Williams.

To Benjamin De Casseres

Wed. Evening—April 14, 1920

DEAR BEN:

You are certainly good to take all the bother over my "case." I'm suffering and horribly from intercostal neuritis, and can about get through the night's chores and no more. I can't think of anything that will lighten your burden. I'm sorry to say Invent! I trust to your imagination. "Steeplejack" is printed since Sept., 1919. Printers' strike held it up from the Christmas holidays, and, as it is in two big vols., 700 pp. illustrated, it goes over till Oct., 1920. I wrote a novel of 78,000 words last summer about New York artistic life; it, too, is delayed. It may be published next Spring. My *first* real novel—at the age of 59 I wrote it with a pen. It may be mildly described as "frank." But nothing wicked! Just spun out a portrait in black and white and purple. Your phrasing will do the rest. This is a rotten note, but I'm ill and grouchy. Uncle Uric is here. (I wrote "urine" and *he* is also here. I have a bad case of diabetes advanced. No cure. I may last till 93, not more.) So pardon my summary of personal news, and again thanks!

As ever,

Ben De Casseres.   JIM.

By all means go to Frisco, Ben, your pen will be a power in any field you elect.

To Henry B. Fuller

Westminster Court
Brooklyn, N. Y.
1618 Beverly Road
April 18, 1920

MY DEAR OLD FRIEND FULLER:

Suffering from intercostal neuritis and diabetes—
a bad case—I couldn't acknowledge your gift. I
do so now. I shall read it next week—as soon as the
opera season ends. I hope it is not a last opus. Do
you ever see Jules Bois—a remarkable writer, ver-
satile, poetic, and in satanic lore profound! I hope
he is not ill; he, too, suffers from the hellish visits of
Uncle Uric of accursed activities.

I may go to London in June, but, frankly, I care
less for travel than I did, J'ai mes soixante ans! I'm
doing Henry James' Letters for the May *Bookman;*
also the hideous musical season for the July *Century.*
But I'm ill—for the first time in precisely 50 years.

Cordially,

H. B. Fuller.   JAMES HUNEKER.

To H. L. Mencken

1618 Beverly Road
Brooklyn, May 5/20

DEAR MENCK:

Thank you for sending me the Munich blatt. (I
only wish I were there now.) Lola Lorme sent me

a copy. She translated the "Chopin"—which has
won "golden" opinions (and gold buys "marks"
over there), because they think Hun-aker is German.
Chase of *Times* can't use a critical note from Munch-
ner *Neusta Nachrichting*. April 3, '20 "going" for
the translation because she mixed up trommel and
tympanum. Serves her right. But the funniest thing
of all was the fact that George Müller the publisher—
died in Dec., 1918—sent me 1,000 mks during the
war—but before 1917—as my moiety for six mos.
royalty. What perfectly infernal bounty! It must
have been propaganda!!! Hal, my lad, at last I'm a
sick man. It's been due years ago—diabetes. My
father always warned me not to bet my kidneys
against the brewery; but I did. I've lost! Doc Williams says I may live till I'm gone, but I'll never cross
the 95 years line. I've not had a drink since April,
1919—yet I'm suffering from neuritis in the stomach.
A gong! Karlsbad is recommended (and pilsner 40
miles away), but the *World* wishes me to "do" London & Paris for the next 6 mos. And I loathe the
idea. The point just now is—how long will I last
with my guts full of darting buzzards! It's curable.
But when! God damn it. Did you see my "go" dog
joke? Not a critic saw it till a woman—also a critic
—asked. Are "go" dogs only male? She knew the
tail made g. and the cipher was the anus—go. But
the female? That's the circumflex over the o I
answered. I'm ill, but I like to enlighten well mean-

ing ——. How is George? "Bedouins" is a best seller! At last. H. Bell Wright, I have you! With regards.

JIM, the Penman.

H. L. Mencken.

To Dr. T. C. Williams

1618 Beverly Road
Brooklyn, N. Y.
May 15/20

DEAR DOCTOR:

After several days amelioration and comparative freedom from pain, I had a bad day at home yesterday, and took 6 or 8 pills—always one at a time—to no effect. I drink hot water before breakfast; it seems to alleviate the nasty little spasms; but it has occurred to me that the last box of pills you sent me by mail are larger pellets than the first box you gave me at the office. However, this may be imagination. The Unchristian Scientists say there is no pain— it's all in the mind! I take the after meals pellets regularly—I wound up last night with a brief, but brilliant indigestion of which I summarily rid myself with soda-mints. I'm pelleted to death— like a golfing course, Mencken writes me—consolingly—that diabetes originates in the pancreas, not in the kidneys. I'll say it ends in the *pissoir*. What is the Allan Treatment? I can't get over, hence these words. The chief thing now seems to be a profound disturbance in the digestive tract; in other words, my food doesn't assimilate, imperfect metabolism. So I'm dieting. No sweets or fruits; gone the bananas. Water, too, is a revolting beverage. The *World* wishes me to try Bath, England; mild, diaretic waters—gout, kidneys, rheumatism, stomach, etc. Do you know anything of its therapeutic qualities— it is famous as a watering-place for centuries. My appetite, bowels, thirst, nerves are unusual. I'm not working hard. But I fancy the trip for 5 or 6 weeks in London, with 4 weeks at Bath, ought to do us both good. We are scheduled to go when—when we can get a steamer, and when there is room to be had in a London hotel, two difficult propositions just now. The nearest date is August 28: and the *World* would like me to be in London June 15. It can't be done!

Please Tom, send me by mail a fresh box of the first neuralgia pills. I'm nearly half-way through the last box, and I don't like aspirin. I'll be in to see you before June 1st. At present I think I have gall-stones, dyspepsia a large and intelligent tumor on the heart, a peristaltic rib, a floating erection, and a most plentiful lack of graftian vesicle, etc., etc. I'd better see a preacher. Yours hypochondriachally, from Josio and your old pal.

JAMES.

Dr. T. C. Williams.

To Benjamin De Casseres

Westminster Court
Brooklyn, N. Y.
June 14, 1920

DEAR BEN:

Thank you for your letter. Yes, I read your amazing remarks in the *Post*: mine, at least, are orthodox. My God what's the E. P. coming to? Blasphemy, Sir! The *Musician* I heard about, but as they don't sell on the stands, L. or Sub., I can't get a copy, and they didn't send me one. I blush with embarrassment in advance. You certainly are generous with an aged pal. "Steeplejack" will be sent to your residence. I'm neuralgic—in the guts. We sail June 26. Baltic for London, where I am assigned for 4 mos. work for the *World*. I'm poor—again, so I couldn't go any place if not *sent*—which means expenses paid. Incidentally I shall take a *kur* at Bath for my diabetes. Not a drink since 15 months! Oh boy! First at the bar when Ambrose Channel (3 mile limit) is reached. "Istar," impossible in English, appears in French.* Keep this dark, especially the title! I hope your Missus is well and unhappy, the latter I'm sure of. Don't I know her man— the veritable begetter of household squabs and squabbles! To be unhappy is to achieve your per-

* "Painted Veils" ("Istar") has not been translated into French.

sonality. No more self-satisfied, greasy happiness
for me. I write the word.

And money! ⎤
And booze! ⎬ The Big 3
And fornication! ⎦

Also illusions (when your teeth and testicles begin
to go.) However, yours are unwrung, let the galled
jades wear suspensories. Goodbye till Nov. European address same old Brown, Shipley & Co.

Stories begin in *World* first August. Regards
from house to house!

As ever,

JIM.

Benjamin De Casseres.

To Dr. T. C. Williams

1618 Beverly Road
Brooklyn, N. Y.
June 15, 1920

DEAR TOM:

I fear I can't get in to say goodbye—so here's how!
We go 26th inst., and if I had known the labor involved in getting passports and the various visés I
should have refused to go. What is the formula of
those pellets you gave me? The pain has almost vanished and I seldom use them, nevertheless, I shall be
away till Nov. and, perhaps—Bath water (more hum-

bug), &c. Send me another box—always asking for boxes!—and God bless you.

As ever,

JAMES.

Dr. T. C. Williams.

To Burton Rascoe

1618 Beverly Road
Brooklyn, N. Y.
June 16/20

MY DEAR MR. RASCOE:

Your letter dropped from the clouds. How the hell—pardon my impetuosity—did you get hold of that mss.? I am glad you did, for no man in the dry land of freedom I prefer when it comes to critical opinion; nevertheless, I think you must have been, you are, too flattering. No book, no matter what the length of its incubation, can be of art that is actually written in 7 weeks, less 2 days. I did this with a pen. A hateful task, but I was ill with a leaky bladder, on the water wagon and pain, with tea as a chaser, drove my pen at top speed. Thanks in re: cigarettes. It is a palpable slip. The motor cars were in existence at the period—1900. As to the expurgation, it is feasible. The book is really a scenario. I may write the play.* So I'll have to "purify!" You are, my dear chap, more than welcome to that page. Really you make me begin to

think "Istar" (not "Painted Veils," a subtitle) is
worth while. Again with thanks for your letter.
                    I am sincerely,
Burton Rascoe.   JAMES HUNEKER.

Explanatory Note:
  Mr. Huneker referred to the manuscript of "Painted
Veils." In going over the manuscript, I noted some errors,
which I either corrected in the text or wrote about to Mr.
Huneker. In one part of the book he had said several
times that the hero did not smoke, and belied the statement
by having this same hero relish Turkish cigarettes. He had
the title of Remy de Gourmont's *Physique de l'Amour* as
Physique d'Amour and attributed an epigram to Stendhal
which really originated with Baudelaire. These I corrected.
I called attention to the "high powered motor car" as a
probable anachronism; and even though he countered that
motor cars were in existence in 1900, I doubt if they were
high powered and capable of being driven at the speed he
has it driven in the novel.
                              BURTON RASCOE.

                    To Maurice Speiser

                         1618 Beverly Road
                         Brooklyn, N. Y.
                         June 16, 1920

DEAR SPEISER:
  Congratulations from the Hunekers to the
Speisers! The worst is over. Cheer up. After
twenty years there is not much more to find out about

each other. Even that beauty spot which every woman has concealed about her person—is definitely located, excites no more interest, though in the morgue it is always a safe means of identification. Pardon my enthusiasm.

We sail June 26 on the *Baltic* for London. I shall write weekly on life and the seven arts jointly for the Sunday *World* which is sending me over with the Missus. In Sept. we go to Bath for a cure. I'm ill. Neuritis, overwork, bored with music. No book on modern or old composers for me. "Steeple-jack" out on Sept. 15.

Our regards to your adorable Martha Washington. (Ha! said the suspicious husband, gloomily! So that's what he means with his beauty spot) and to the boys and to Maurice himself—not forgetting her brother.

As ever, cordially,
JAMES HUNEKER.

Maurice Speiser.

To Benjamin De Casseres

Sat., June 19/20

DEAR BEN:

I'm obliged to you for the M. M. which arrived yesterday. I shan't thank you for the story—I couldn't. Talk about my Mariolatry (Garden)! But, unlike Mary, I shall never be able to "live up to" a tithe of the things you say of me with that wizard pen of yours. What a memory is yours. After you wrote it I recall that first encounter at Jack's—my brother John, who was of the company. What golden nights, drab dawns, and yet what a spur rum was to our galled jades! What's the use, it's all over! You bring back the atmosphere in an evocation that might be Klingsor's—but a Klingsor with balls. Like the man in the story who shot himself I have nothing to say. I'm overbalanced but happy.

As ever,

Benjamin De Casseres.

To Mme. Frida Ashforth

Sunday, June 20, 1920

MY DEAR YOUNG FRIEND:

You are too sweet for anything. We should accept that lovely invitation in a jiffy but the *World* is sending me to London and the Missus goes along, so we shall put off the visit for a year. I'm not very well —neuritis in my side; in anglais—gout in the guts. Too much uric acid, too much work. So I'll take a *kür* at Bath, England in Sept. But first I shall write of the London season for the Sunday *World* beginning first Sunday in August. Home in November. We sail next Saturday, June 26th, on the S. S. Baltic. Incredible are the prices for staterooms. Of course,

Frida, the *World* pays all expenses, else I should have
to rusticate here all summer. We hope your vege-
tables will lower H. C. L. and that your rugged health
—what else is it?—will endure. In Oct., early, you
will get copy of "Steeplejack" (2 vols.) containing
some pictures you gave me of Jean & Salvini, &c. I'm
worn out—no vacation since 1913. Goodbye and love
from Josia and your old pal.

Mme. Frida Ashforth.

To T. R. Smith

Hotel Rubens
Buckingham Palace Road, S.W.
London, Aug. 4, 1920

DEAR TOM:

It has been steadily pouring water from leaden
skies since July 1st, so home we go. Don't send
any letters, etc., here but to my old Brooklyn address
(1618 Beverly Road). We expect to be there about
Aug. 23rd next. I had hoped for news of "Istar"*
before this. I fancy you had no serious intention of
publishing it but thought the story might furnish
reading for some of those many girls of yours—Summer girls, of course. I'm sorry if this is the case, as
I should like to get the load off my mind. After the

* Title changed later to "Painted Veils."

book appears in French I'll burn the English version, but shan't bowdlerize it. Greetings from

JIM.

Bossomo's is Italian, not French. It's good.
T. R. Smith.

To Horace B. Liveright

1618 Beverly Road
Brooklyn, N. Y.
Sep. 2, 1920

MY DEAR LIVERIGHT:

I tried to get you on the phone Tuesday and Wednesday but in vain, so I am dropping you a line to tell you that I've been marooned in Flatbush since last Sunday, thanks to the damnable strike on the B. R. T. But things look brighter and I hope matters will be adjusted so that I can get over to see you early next week without incurring the danger of a broken head. I've read the proof carefully and found it clean copy, so my corrections are light; only changes in spelling and absolutely necessary. Consequently the corrections on page proof will be nil; really only to verify corrections. Otherwise I shouldn't bother with them.

Now—as to the change in the title.

When the expurgated volume publicly appears I shall use my original title, "Istar: Daughter of Sin." But for this forthcoming private edition I don't like

"The Seven Veils," for, apart from the fact that it is not new, being used everywhere from ballet to opera, from book titles to vaudeville, I think it flat, commonplace, and not sufficiently arresting; nor is it pertinent to the contents of the book—"The Seven Gates" would be closer but that, too, is not eye-catching. Let me propose something far more striking and dramatic: *i. e.* "The Seven Deadly Sins."

The sins are frequently referred to, besides there is snap and suggestion of wickedness in the title. And it is altogether novel, so novel that it might serve, if you see fit, to bring out a public edition of the book. What do you think? I'm sure Tom Smith will like it, and you too (I'll fetch over proof with me when I see you). As to the business side, we can settle that in an hour over the soup and coffee. Monday is a holiday, but I'll be free Tuesday, Thursday, Friday—not Wednesday next week.

The money, as Smith suggests in a letter which has been returned here from London, can be paid in two instalments, but really I think you might bring out 1,500 copies easily. As to the later deodorized publication, that would be arranged without much palaver. In a word—wait till we meet. I hope Tom can be with us.

As ever, sincerely yours,

JAMES HUNEKER.

Horace B. Liveright.

To Alden March

Sunday, Sept. 19, 1920

My Dear Alden:

Your letter gave me great pleasure, and I'm obliged to you for your practical interest in "Steeplejack." If anyone again asks you about the dedication just tell them for me that you are to blame for the book, and you alone. So much for Buckingham —off with his head! "Painted Veils" is a sequel to "Steeplejack"; in it the suppressed "complexes," as the Freudians say, come to the surface; but I didn't write it because I wished to say unpleasant things about unpleasant subjects, but simply because of the story, rather the three stories—there are three heroines, all of them hot and hollow. I hope you will like the novel—my first, written the summer of 1919 in 7 breathless weeks. I enclose letter from Charlie Lincoln which may interest you; read and destroy. C. M. L. has gone over to the *Sun-Herald*. But, alas, there is always Frank Munsey! We miss L. in the *World*. Had a horrible wet—rain, not rum —time in England. Glad I'm home. I wrote 25,000 words in 5 weeks and nothing to write about. I'll be over sooner than you think. I hope to sit down at Dooner's with the old gang. How is my Beamish boy? And how are you? You didn't speak of your health. I hope your guts are behaving. N. Y. is

simply hell afloat after London. Noise!! The
Missus sends her regards.

As ever, your old pal,

JAMES HUNEKER.

Alden March.

To Mme. Frida Ashforth

Wed. Evening, Sept. 22, 1920

MY DEAR FRIDA:

Your welcome letter just read. I'm glad you are
well in all the *tohn-bohn* of our awful New York life.
You should have had "Steeplejack" long ago. I
fancy that it was delivered by hand, not by mail, as
these are 2 volumes very heavy and richly got up.
I'm writing in this mail to *Scribner's* and it will be sent
you by parcel post. If you don't get the book by, say
next Tuesday or Wednesday, write me again. I particularly don't want you to buy the volumes, not because they cost $7.50 (edition de luxe, remember;
the Scribners pay me a big compliment), but because
you are my oldest and dearest friend, you are in the
narrative, and two pictures—in fact, 3, one of the
young Patti and the two de Reszkes—you gave me.
It's a matter of sentiment, Frida. There is to be a
review of "Steeplejack" by Mencken in the N. Y.
Evening Post next Saturday.

Curiously enough your letter found me at my
desk here correcting the final page proof of "Painted

Veils" in which you figure as "Frida Ash,"
taut simple. Liveright, with whom I made a fairly
good contract—I'm not giving away any of my books,
I can't afford it—told me that he recognized the portrait at once. You go straight through the story,
which is not obscene, nor blasphemous. Its merits,
if any, are its frankness and character dissection.
Naturally, you will get a complimentary copy from
me; the book is expensive, at least $10, later it will
fetch bigger prices, but neither Liveright nor I will
benefit; there are only 1,200 numbered and signed
copies; another de luxe. And the printers may stop
publication, so if you do show enclosed circular to
any of your friends—as you so kindly suggested—
tell them that the book is not to be advertised nor
indeed talked about. For you, unprejudiced and ac-
quainted with good French and German literature,
the story will not offend. It is not a smutty story.
It's truthful. The motto on the title page is "Le
Verita tonta nue." The New York, artistic and Bo-
hemian of 1895-1905, is the theme. The old Felix
hotel, your music room on 18th St. These old land-
marks are described. But it is the characterization
that will, I hope, interest you. We hope to call on
you when you come up here from?—Jozio sends her
love.

As ever,

Jim.

To Dr. T. C. Williams

Flatbush—adjacent to all Cemeteries
Wed., Sep. 29/20

MY DEAR TOM:

Yours must be the first cheque for P. V.; and I'm greatly obliged for the compliment, yet I'm returning it as I have nothing to do with the business end—you had better send it to H. B. Liveright, 105 West 40th St., and mark your letter "personal." Sorry to put you to all this trouble. Yes, Mencken's notice is amusing, but it is not precise. The book is a serious study of character; the so-called "Rabelaisian" episodes are, with several exceptions, clinical, not obscene. You will judge for yourself. Did you get "Steeplejack"? I ordered a copy for you. Please let me know if it came—and how. It is a success from the start, simply because it is human and sincere. Mencken likes "Painted Veils" better; so do I. But "Steeplejack" is for the general public; the other book is for the few who understand. I wrote 25,000 words for the N. Y. *World* in London, where it rained for 40 days without cessation. Cold, wretchedly damp and dreary. Bath registered 32° and under water and slush. You can't take a *kur* in a bath tub! So I drank pilsner, real, imported from Pilsen, 2½ percent alcohol and it did me more good than the damned sugar water in this land. I'm glad to announce the divorce of Miss Prep— from

Mr. Glans-P— (another hyphenated bastard), which occurred in London last July. The pair had been deeply attached to each other since 1913—also in London. At all events I am no longer suffering from a painful and embarrassing adhesion. No wonder it was difficult to get "expansive." That means, I suppose, that my sugar index is not so high. I'm cured of the neuritis, eat heartily, and glad I'm again on a watery basis. The wine, ale and beer in London is on too low an alcoholic base to taste; besides, I feel better without it. Less heated and nervous. No more depressed awakenings; nevertheless, I own, I'm against prohibition. Look at the Sunday *World* supplement next Sunday, Oct. 3rd, article entitled "The Return of the Native." I soak the puritan gang. Josephine, is, or rather was, well on arrival, since then she has had nothing but troubles, no servant, disagreeable work. I take off the ice in the morning and curse the whole rotten politics that has made servants better than their masters. But I believe the tide has set in the other, the right way again. We both hope you are in fine fettle after your vacation. I'll be in early next month with my reform —p—s "enbonteille." Now, don't forget to let me know about "Steeplejack" copy.

With regards, as ever yours,

JAMES HUNEKER.

Dr. T. C. Williams.

To T. R. Smith

1618 Beverly Road
Brooklyn, N. Y.
Sep. 29, 1920

DEAR TOM:

Did Scribner's send you "Steeplejack"? I hope so, and I hope you will read the chapters devoted to Shaw & Conrad & Moore in vol II: the letters of G. B. S. alone would sell the book—which is a success from the start. Do you know anything? That essay for the *Century*, of which we spoke when I last saw you. "The Lost Art of Leisure" I can't write just now because I haven't the leisure! What a joke. Not leisure enough in Gotham to write about leisure.

By the way, Tom, does that "friend" of yours wish to part with "Fanny H.," which you lent me last spring? I'll pay a reasonable price. Let me know, and also let me know about "Steeplejack."

With regards,

T. R. Smith.   JIM.

To John Quinn

1618 Beverly Road
Brooklyn, N. Y.
Oct. 6/20

MY DEAR JOHN:

Thank you for your letter. I wished to be clear in my mind, for as I told Liveright, I shan't assume any responsibility. The ennui of a trial would drive me to London. But as they are going into the matter open-eyed there is no need of worry on my part.

Too bad about the Joyce book. I've had charming letters from Wickersham and Judge Ward. I saw Ward last week, met him and Judge Hough. He was extremely cordial and spoke to me of my father—which surprised me, for it is at least 40 years since we met.

I'm not a prime chop. I miss a warming glass of claret. My circulation isn't good. The diabetes seems to have withdrawn its sugary forces temporarily. I hope you are well. But the noise and stinking vulgarity of New York are distinctly depressing. I took a crack at the nuisances last Sunday in the *World*; and lost my temper, which is a mistake. I've just received a letter from Mencken. Roosevelt and my rampant Americanism are to blame for his extraordinary act of critical radicalism in the *Post*. Now he is sorry he wrote it. I should worry. Nevertheless—in next Sunday's *World* I've taken a hack at such reviewing.

With love from both,

JAMES.

John Quinn.

To H. L. Mencken

1618 Beverly Road
Brooklyn, N. Y.
Oct. 6/20

DEAR MENCK:

My hay fever, not a severe attack, discouraged writing when I arrived from wet London. I had a hard summer, rain for 40 days and 25,000 words in 5 weeks for the *World*. No vacation. No "kur." I should have gone to Karlsbad. But the imported pilsner at the old *Gambrinus* in London, genuine pilsner from Bohemia, "cured" me; at least, it expelled the sugar from my blood. As you say, I'm doomed to live 105 years. Lincoln will write you. No, I stay with the *World*. I like the berth, though I miss C. M. L. As to "Steeplejack," naturally I'm sorry you don't see it, but what's a book review between pals? I'm also sorry Roosevelt and Towse were my chief offences. I can't recall any 100 per cent Americanism talk, and as for Towse, remember that I'm comparing him to W. Winter 35 years ago. He was always fairer and saner than Winter. He didn't call Sarah Bernhardt a harlot. You forget that *S.* is a book of the past, not dealing with the present. However, no bones are broken. You have been so kind to me for years that I blush to write you

the above.   By the way, every line in the 2 vols. appeared in the *Press*; nothing was "saved" for the
printed volumes; in fact, the boot is on the other leg:
I threw out three chapters on certain art collections
in Phila. and S—— would not stand for a line in one
of the Shaw letters referring to buggery in England
and flagellation among the sailors and soldiers. This
line appeared in the *Press*—in Rodman Wanamaker's
newspaper.   The joy of it!   I'm sorry you made no
mention of the Shaw letters.   They are a gold mine
and are selling the book.   And that closes the matter, Hal, except that I shall have some fun in the
World next Sunday over your review simply to stop
the mouths of condoling friends who seem to think
we are at loggerheads.   It makes me ill, the small-
ness of people.   I am, if you please, a good American, even though I criticise my country; rather, criticise the mutts who are running it.   I printed the
Roosevelt chapter for the express purpose of the
speech he made to me—intended for Wilson—about
the *Lusitania* incident.   But, of course, you didn't
read the book, so there's an end on it.

Cordially, with regards to George.

As ever,

JIM.

H. L. Mencken.

To John Quinn

1618 Beverly Road
Brooklyn, N. Y.
Oct. 10, 1920

MY DEAR JOHN:

If the glass is set fair, *i. e.* if it is not raining felines will next Saturday afternoon, or Saturday eight days later, suit your convenience for a meeting? If it is agreeable I should like our rencontre to be three, as you suggested in an earlier letter.

I'm thoroughly disheartened by the hostile atmosphere of this vulgar and sinister city. Depressed would be a more fitting word. I look forward with horror to the music season, when I shall write several hundred thousand words, useless killing, during the 6 months' season. Am I never to escape the slough, the trough, of daily journalism? I'm searching, lantern in hand, a Mæcenas. If only I could go to France, to Southern France, and write the few books still in me, and the one play! I could live there one-half as cheaply as I do here. And then the atmosphere—the escape from this noisy inferno. However, let us meet and I'll make you my unwilling confessor. I'm well, but I'll end in neurasthenia. Life is a noise.

As ever,

JAMES.

John Quinn.

To Maurice Speiser

1618 Beverly Road
October 10,—20

DEAR SPEISER MAURICE:

Thank you for your kind inquiries. A rotten trip —though *real* pilsner is sold across the bars in London. But too much rain. Yes, I heard the *Press* is sold. I thought at once of Ben Glazer. What is he doing? Thank him for the beautiful notice of "Steeple Smoke"! For me he is a loyal friend. No Atlantic this season. We are both better. I am due to live 105 years. How is your brood? Tell Martha, the Washington, we often speak of her, I dreamed of her in London. Not a co-respondent's dream, but a true Irish one; she offered me booze! I lunched with Judge Henry Galbraith Ward Sunday —my first and only law preceptor. How we joked over my legal studies. Busy! phew! "Painted Veils" will soon be published. Another row attends.

Give our regards to the Missus and the boys, not forgetting Morrie!

As ever,

JAMES HUNEKER.

Maurice Speiser.

To Benjamin De Casseres

Oct. 17, 1920, Bklyn., N. Y.

DEAR BEN:

I hope you will see it through—that movie scheme
for, believe me, there is nothing in the book illusion.
No money and press clippings won't pay the rent.
Stick, my lad!

As for the other matter—also nothing. But do
please read again that article of mine, carefully.
You may find much to commend it as a specimen of
not only turning the other cheek but also of polishing
off a question without raising one's voice. At least,
that is the critical opinion of experts, critical and lay.
However, what's the use of finding fault with anyone
who disagrees! Life is too brief.

Cordially,

JIM.

Benjamin De Casseres.

To Richard Bach

N. Y. *World*, Oct. 17, 1920

DEAR DICK:

Glad to hear from you, gladder to know you have
landed. I hope A. M. will come here, yet I think
Phila. is a more comfortable, a more human place to
live in. Has Magers left P.? The movies or plays are
decidedly better investments than writing words. I

regret my past performances, and look forward with
horror to another season of musical noises.

Mencken is all right, Richard. His notice won't
do any harm; besides, I must take the good with the
bad or vice versa. Menck has proved his friendship
in a hundred ways. And you mustn't forget that he
read "Painted Veils" before "Steeplejack"—of
which it is the sequel. No wonder *S* seemed tame, as
it really is (I didn't wish the publishers to go to jail).
Good luck, old chap, and give my regards to Jim
Craven and to Mrs. Craven, if you should ever see
her. I hope Mrs. Beamish is well and that the off-
spring is growing—*not* the family. Safety first!

Cordially,

Richard Beamish.   JAMES HUNEKER.

To Horace B. Liveright

Tuesday *Dies Iræ,*
Oct. 27, 1920

DEAR LIVERIGHT:

Of all the God-damnable set of imbeciles—but I
choke with rage, I sputter, I fume, I stutter, I foam
(why in the name of the Mommser didn't your printer
send me enclosed bastard or false title page; it is from
the proof sheets in book form you sent me), instead
of a sheet of 4, which made a bundle that sprawled
over our floor—3 bundles to be exact. I didn't mind
the signing as much as the opening and closing of the

huge parcels. We are not floorwalkers, or people who put up parcels. My poor wife got on her knees to tie up the bundles, for we feared the soft paper would crinkle and instead of putting the sheets—1,300—in a box so they would retain their shape and not crease—no, the idiots wrapped paper about the matter. When I first saw what they dumped with a crash I really fancied the entire book had been sent. Jessas! I signed my full name because it is only playing fair with the subscribers; even to get my wife to have signed in my place would not have been fair. But, Horace, never again, do you hear, young fellow. Five of my precious hours have I wasted writing my sickening signature and 1,225 times, the other 75 not being required, as enclosed letter shows. I never balked at one. But I cursed you all; *i. e.* I put the Irish curse on Tom. He will lose his manhood for at least 48 hours—poor fish! Serves him right for suggesting that "James" (oh I shudder, I vomit that hideous name—1,225 James's. Shamus in Irish, Shamus in Yiddish, and in Hebrew Shamus Hanuchah!) Remember, my boy, if you sell an English edition we rubber-stamp it, else hire a policeman or a motorman to forge it. I shall certainly expect compensation for my awful day of wrath; compensation, if not in cold cash, at least in publisher's courtesy. Which means you must send with my card copies of the book to Joe Conrad, Saltus, Havelock Ellis, George Moore and Arnold Bennett. Sure, say you. You and Tommy must lunch with me some-time—that is, as soon as the book is out and the opera season begins. I've written the Arbor press people to send for their paper on Friday. Ring them up and insist. It's my only day home.

Cordially,

J. H.

Otherwise James Huneker.

To John Quinn

Thursday, Oct. 28, 1920

DEAR JOHN:

Your letter greatly relieved me, I'm getting shady on proper names, and on dates I'm never sure; but color, form—tone! My God! If I forget color then my memory is gone. Nevertheless, it was a nat-ural mistake for McBride to make. Van Gogh painted a dozen self-portraits. Yours is better than Montross's I've read Edith Wharton's "Age of Innocence." Pale, prim, proper, anæmic, yet—pure rot—I'm reading "Captain Macedome's Daughter" of McFee—Très Joseph Conrad thus far—and I've "Potterism" on my desk. And yesterday I signed 1,200 copies of "Painted Whores" or some such title. My work as musical scavenger begins Thursday, Nov. 4—next week. Love from both.

As ever,

John Quinn.

JAMES.

To Benjamin De Casseres

Nov. 3, 1920

DEAR BEN:

Only a line to tell you, *entre nous*, that I was astonished at the reviewing of "Painted Veils" in the *E. Post* last Saturday (the *Literary Review*). It was a breach of confidence I have been told as publicity is the last thing we want. All this because I don't want you to think that some one got a copy and you didn't. You, naturally, would be first. I'll see that you get a complimentary copy when the book appears —in a few weeks perhaps Liveright will give you one now—but not for review. How are you! Musical season begins tomorrow for me. Six months wasted time, temper, nerves, over piddling poddlers and slithering pianists. How long, O Lord!   Regards from.   JIM.

B. De Casseres.

To Benjamin De Casseres

Nov. 10, 1920

DEAR BEN:

Glad to hear from you. I'm ill. Vertigo—falling down all over shop. Toxenia, or what the hell —auto-intoxication. Truth is I'm worn to the bone with work to keep body and soul together—working

for the landlord and food! I'm on strict diet.
"Painted Whores" is not yet out—by Thanksgiving.
Can't make any engagement this or next week.
Barber shop is in full operation. Music! Anyhow,
you lunch with me. I saw you first. Keep at the
real—else starve in Flatbush as I'm doing—not food,
but spiritually.

In haste, as ever,

JIM.

Benj. De Casseres.

To Horace B. Liveright

Westminster Court
1618 Beverly Road
Brooklyn, N. Y.
Nov. 23, 1920

DEAR LIVERIGHT:

What's become of P. V.? I'm assailed every day
by inquiries. I heard indirectly from London that
P. V. is soon to be published there. Is this true? If
it be—and I hope it is—I wish to suggest three typographical changes on the sheets. Last line, page
186, a bad "p" not to be found in the corrected proof.
It happened during the revised printing. On page
272, seventh line from bottom of page there is "or" instead of "nor"; not much of an error, yet it should
be corrected. The most annoying "break" is on the
last page of the book, second line from last. "Lamp"

should read "map."   This is all the more of an eye-
sore because it makes nonsense of the sentence and
also because I must have passed it.   Can't it be
changed if there be another edition for New York
or for London?   Don't forget that I am to get down
here 12 free copies—don't send me signed ones—and
that you promised to mail free for me a half-dozen
extra copies for my bother in signing the sheets to
Arnold Bennett, Joseph Conrad, Havelock Ellis,
George Moore and Edgar Saltus.   I'll give you the
addresses when you are ready.   And how about that
cheque (for I presume the book has been over sub-
scribed.   Can't you send in the entire amount in one
cheque?)   Then we could talk over another book I
have in mind.   I'm so rushed by opera, &c., I
haven't had a chance to see you.

Cordially,
JAMES HUNEKER.

Horace B. Liveright.

To Horace B. Liveright

Westminster Court
1618 Beverly Road
Brooklyn, N. Y.
Dec. 3, 1920

DEAR H. B.:
  You will be surprised to learn that only this Friday
morning I opened the P. V. package which came last

night and saw the book. So please pardon what must have seemed indifference or impoliteness in not acknowledging your courtesy. Tom's enthusiasm over the general get-up, appearance and quality of the book is justified. It is truly a stunning volume and I'm all "het up" at the thought of such a beautiful garb. I sent a circular to my old friend, Senator Henry Cabot Lodge, this morning. If he should subscribe try to dig him up a volume some place; he is an epicure of literature.

Sincerely,
JAMES HUNEKER

Horace B. Liveright.

To Henry B. Fuller

Westminster Court
Brooklyn, N. Y.
Dec. 19, 1920

MY DEAR MR. FULLER:

I can't help telling you that after "The Chevalier," which was a marking-stone in my development, nothing you have written has so stirred me as "Bertram Cope's Year." I've read it three times, the last in London during a rainy spell last July. Its portraiture and psychological strokes fill me with envy and also joy. *Ca y est,* I said to myself. And Chicago! It is as desolate, your dissection, as a lunar landscape. We are like that, not like Whitman's Camerades and his joyful junk. Why do you speak of your last book! You are only beginning, you implacable Stendhal of the lake! My first novel, written in my 60th year, is a fragment; if I had a copy I'd send it to you. But you won't like it. It's too bitter and cynicism is always unreal. I had to get it off my chest and when I tell you that I've rung some changes on the pleasing theme of Lesbianism you may be shocked. The book is privately printed at a prohibitive price and sold like the first oysters of the season. Its title is "Painted Veils," but the imps of the perverse down here call it, not without reason, "Painted Tails." On this note I fear I must close.

In all friendship, I am yours,

JAMES HUNEKER.

H. B. Fuller.

To H. L. Mencken

Beverly Road
Brooklyn, N. Y.
Dec. 27/20

DEAR HAL:

You will pardon my silence when I tell you that, literally, I haven't had the time or the strength to write you. I say "strength" because while I really don't write more than 5 or 6,000 words a week, the hideous subway travel from here to the *World*, to the opera, to Carnegie or Aeolian Hall, consumes my

vitality. My legs have aged more quickly than my
skull—anyhow I hope so. I was disappointed to hear
from H. B. Liveright that your copy of P. V. had
been sent without a line of mine. (I wrote in
George's book, thanks to Tom Smith.) So I enclose
a "fitting tribute," as they say when a Bishop dies at
the house of his masseuse from the shock superin-
duced by an unexpected ejaculation. Also a half
dozen cards for the other books—I sincerely hope
you haven't saved more than six. I shan't assault
your sensibilities with belated expressions of gratitude, but you may permit me to remind *you* of the
debt I owe you. I never thanked you for the advance
notice of P. V.—which is kicking up the dust here and
in Chicago, much to my consternation—but I do so
now. I don't agree altogether with your dictum that
the form is "loose"; to me it is "tight," indeed, pain-
fully crampled by the use of the Istar device of Seven
Gates, &c.; also because I deliberately adopted the
elliptical method of Flaubert as in his "Education."
Furthermore, I planned a three voice fugue with an
elaborate coda—the 3 girls as themes. "Painted
Tails," as they have rechristened the damnably jejune
book. So much for that. And thank you for the
S. S. notice of "Steeplejack," especially the allusion
to my mother. As to the decoration joke I'm sorry
I must spoil it for the simple reason I never possessed
a rosette of the society.* Have never attended their

* National Society of Arts and Letters.

meetings or banquets. I allowed myself to be
elected to please certain people remotely connected
with the publishing business. You understand!
This is not an apology but an explanation, so pray
consider it confidential. But I did sport once or
twice, though not in a barroom—there are no more
barrooms here—a purple rosette or decoration of the
order of merit awarded me for services to French art
and literature. And that's a different thing. I soon
discarded it as every one now-a-days displays orders,
decorations, &c. In London last summer I occasionally wore a button sent to me by the Bürgermeister of
Vienna, conferring upon me the freedom of that unhappy city. I did this for the sake of sheer paradox;
besides it was a touchstone for Austrian and German
waiters masking as Swiss in the Gambrinus and other
bier halle. I wish you could have seen the look of
mingled awe and astonishment when they saw the
button. Ach! Prev Jessus, sin sie Oestreicher.
And those are the only two decorations I own.
I don't blame you for wanting to shoot me if
I had worn the other button—by the way, this is
the first I knew there was one. I only received a receipt on ordinary note paper for my annual dues of
$5. If I should ever have the luck to see you in the
flesh again I must show you my "Chopin" in German. A wonderfully got up book, illustrations
galore. It appeared in 1914. The war drove the
publisher, Georg Müller of Munich into bankruptcy

and later, typhoid fever killed the poor chap, who was a forward-looking, even adventurous man, handling such dynamite as Wedekind, &c. He sent me 1,000 marks—early in 1917, when the mark was normal. The book went into a 2nd edition in 1920. But the mark!

With best wishes for a pleasant and prosperous New Year—merry or happy are absurd words now-a-days in this land—I am,

As ever, my dear Menck,

Jim.

H. L. Mencken.

To Nathan Burkan

Westminster Court
Sunday, Jan. 9/21

MY DEAR NATHAN BURKAN:

Herewith I return briefs and affidavits in *re* Ricordi vs. Remick. I shan't be able to give you an affidavit in the case for 3 following reasons: 1st—When I asked a certain high authority on my papers—of course not mentioning names in the matter—I was refused point-blank the necessary permission, as it would involve the name of the paper in question. So that makes it—*ausgeschlossen* from the start. 2nd—It seems to me, after a careful reading of the various arguments, that the ground is completely covered, both in your own statement of actual facts, but also in the comprehensive estimate of Harry Rowe Shelley. I don't know of a single new point that could strengthen your side of the question so completely has Mr. Shelley dealt with it. The summing up is not difficult. (By the way, an error has crept into several of the affidavits: *i.e.*, the key of "Avalon" is *two*, not one tone, below the original.) 3rd—For your private ear. When you showed me the two themes the other day there is a resemblance; but when I examined the Puccini scores (piano and orchestra) and compared them with "Avalon" I found your case considerably weakened; indeed, my dear Burkan, if I may be frank, I don't think the case is a strong one.

Puccini is an Italian, lives in Italy; while the composer or composers of the fox-trot are Americans and *here*. Tweedledum and Tweedledee, the judge will think. I hardly think you have a legal leg to stand on so cleverly is the time camouflaged. But this is the mere surmise of a layman. The chief thing for me is that I can't touch the matter without coming into conflict with my superiors, thereby jeopardizing my position. Naturally the matter is a strictly kept secret *entre nous*. I'm really sorry I can be of no assistance after all the trouble you have taken. Now, may I make a suggestion, just for what it is worth! It is this: Why not ask Henry T. Finck, musical editor of the *Evening Post* (20 Vesey St.; residence, 485 Manhattan Avenue, City?). I'll tell you my reason for suggesting his name. In his "Richard Strauss" (published by Little, Brown & Co.) he recites the facts in the lawsuit instituted by the publishers of Strauss against a young composer named Noren (this in 1907). Noren wrote a symphonic variation called "Kaleidoscope," in which he introduced two themes from the "Heldenleben" of Strauss and crediting him as follows: "To a famous contemporary." Strauss didn't object, but his publishers did (probably incited thereto by the practical Strauss). In section 13 of the copyright law of 1901 it is declared that "In a musical composition it is not permissible to take a recognizable melody from it and incorporate it in a new work." So far, good, but the "melody" proved to be only a "theme" and Strauss & Co. lost their case. However, it is the commentary of Finck—on page 122 of his book—that is the strangest argument against this sort of filching. He recognizes the complications that are bound to arise; altogether, he makes a strong case against the practice and I fancy he might prove a material witness for your side.

For my own part, I'm dubious. The eternal imbecility of mankind is at its flood just now in America. Theft is enthroned. I must not forget to add that I have been a persistent and consistent opponent of Puccini because of his innumerable "appropriations" —notably in "Madame Butterfly," the introduction to which he calmly "swiped" from Smetana's "Bartered Bride" (ask Otto Weil). Naturally, two wrongs don't make a right, but I might be "hoist by my own petard" for Liebling in the *Courier* has often commented on my hostility to the Italian master— Goneff.   Sincerely,

JAMES HUNEKER.

Nathan Burkan.

To George Jean Nathan

Sat. Jan. 15/21

(Pardon my shaky hand!)

MY DEAR GEORGE:

I appreciate your note all the more because Menck told me of your suffering. Really, you shouldn't abuse your eyes by reading P. V.; or, indeed, anything at all. But I'm grateful all the same. In the mail with your letter was another from a prominent and powerful churchman—probably the biggest man in the American hierarchy. It was dated from the Cardinalate at Westminster Cathedral, London. It contained the news that, despite the brutal frankness of the book, no such moral fiction had appeared in our national literature since Hawthorne (pardon the bouquets). And Menck gave the story the first send-off. I shall always be in his debt—and in yours for the encouraging lift. After all, I'm not yet 61 and it's my first fiction! I'll try to do better next time. Horace has proved very friendly. But—there is always some one taking the joy out of life. I'm ill. I'm indoors; though I shall force myself to hear "Louise" today. Vertigo. Tumbling on my face or my arse all over the shop. Cause: eyestrain which affects the stomach. Nausea. Horror of life. Vita sexualis very low indeed. Guts are going. And what with one's teeth, hair, testicles on the wane what is there to live for? Pardon the pessimism. You no doubt suffer more in an hour than I do in a month. Is Mary Garden a super-woman? At last the public will realize her remarkable brain.

Regards to Menck and to you, George.

As ever,

JIM.

George Jean Nathan.

INDEX OF LETTERS

THE END